LLEWELLYN'S 2021

HERBAL
ALMANAC

© 2020 Llewellyn Publications
Llewellyn Publications is a registered trademark of
Llewellyn Worldwide Ltd.

Cover Designer: Kevin R. Brown
Editor: Lauryn Heineman

Interior Art: © Fiona King
Garden plan illustrations on pages 286–87
by Llewellyn Art Department

You can order annuals and books from *New Worlds,*
Llewellyn's catalog. To request a free copy, call 1-877-
NEW WRLD toll-free or visit www.llewellyn.com.

ISBN: 978-0-7387-5482-6
Llewellyn Worldwide Ltd.
2143 Wooddale Drive
Woodbury, MN 55125-2989

Printed in the United States of America

Contents

DIY and Crafts

Plant Profiles

Gardening Resources

Introduction to
Llewellyn's Herbal Almanac

Holistic care for the mind, body, and soul starts in the garden. Gardeners of all skill levels and climates can find common ground in early morning weeding, combating pests, marveling at this year's abundant harvest, and impatiently waiting to plan next year's plot. The work is hard, but the rewards are bountiful. Growing herbs is good for the spirit, and using them in home-cooked meals, remedies, and crafts is clean, healthy, and just plain delicious.

The 2021 edition of the *Herbal Almanac* is a love letter and guidebook to the hands-on application of herbs in our daily lives. With sage advice appealing to novice gardeners and experienced herbalists alike, our experts tap into the practical and historical aspects of herbal knowledge—using herbs to help you connect with the earth, enhance your culinary creations, and heal your body and mind.

In addition to the twenty-four articles written by Master Gardeners, professors, and homesteaders, this book offers reference materials tailored specifically for successful growing and gathering. Use this book to log important dates, draw your garden plan, practice companion planting, find a helpful herbal remedy, and keep track of goals and chores in the personal logbook pages.

Reclaiming our connection to Mother Earth in our own backyards can bring us harmony and balance—and a delicious, healthy harvest. May your garden grow tall and your dishes taste divine!

Note: The old-fashioned remedies in this book are historical references used for teaching purposes only. The recipes are not for commercial use or profit. The contents are not meant to diagnose, treat, prescribe, or substitute consultation with a licensed health-care professional. Herbs, whether used internally or externally, should be introduced in small amounts to allow the body to adjust and to detect possible allergies. Please consult a standard reference source or an expert herbalist to learn more about the possible effects of certain herbs. You must take care not to replace regular medical treatment with the use of herbs. Herbal treatment is intended primarily to complement modern health care. Always seek professional help if you suffer from illness. Also, take care to read all warning labels before taking any herbs or starting on an extended herbal regimen. Always consult medical and herbal professionals before beginning any sort of medical treatment—this is particularly true for pregnant women. Herbs are powerful things; be sure you are using that power to achieve balance.

Llewellyn Worldwide does not participate in, endorse, or have any authority or responsibility concerning private business transactions between its authors and the public.

Growing
and
Gathering

Late-Season Herb Gardening

~ Elizabeth Barrette ~

At the end of the growing season, the tasks of herb gardening change pace. The emphasis shifts from creation to conclusion. Before you start, it's helpful to browse some possibilities. Then make a list of what *must* get done and what you also want to accomplish. Let's take a look at how that works.

What Is Late-Season Herb Gardening?

The nature of late-season herb gardening depends considerably on where you live. Bear in mind that the seasons are *reversed* in the Northern and Southern Hemispheres. That means "autumn" south of the equator happens some time in March, April, May,

or thereabouts. Watch for seasonal cues in your yard to determine the exact timing.

Most people live in what's called a **temperate climate**. It typically has four seasons: spring, summer, autumn, winter. Late-season gardening in this context usually means late summer and early fall. In many places, it spans August and September. Here in the Midwest, I do much of my gardening in September through October when the weather is cool and before it turns frigid.

However, some variation due to climate occurs. The colder the climate overall, the more compressed the seasons become, which is why those in Upper Peninsula Michigan make jokes like "June, July, August, and winter" or "nine months of winter and three months of bad skiing." It is more essential to work fast in such settings, and you shouldn't expect anything to grow over the winter. You may only have a couple of weeks in July and August.

The warmer the climate overall, the more extended the seasons become. In the South, much planting happens in the late season to take advantage of cooling temperatures and because mild winters allow plants to keep growing slowly. You have more time to work in this context, but you also have to contend with plants still growing, so some tasks may need to be repeated. It often spans September, October, and November.

Then there are some completely different climates. The most relevant to herb gardening rely on rain. This can be a four-beat pattern: rainy, dry, rainy, dry. It can be a two-beat pattern: monsoon, not monsoon. Deserts often have a one-beat pattern: it rains very rarely, so that defines a boom of activity and then shortly thereafter the late-season effects arrive, regardless of the time of year. Most places with a rain-driven climate rather than a temperature-driven climate are closer to the equator. However, they all have common caretaking requirements: you have to clean up after the wet season and prepare for the dry season, which means a lot more attention to water management than temperate climates typically require.

Note that many herbs come from a Mediterranean climate, found around the Mediterranean Sea and the west coast of North America, among other places. Also called a **dry summer climate**, it has warm to hot summers with little or no rain followed by wet mild winters. That means you do a majority of your planting either at the beginning or end of the cool wet season, not the warm dry season. Herbs adapted to this cycle may struggle to adjust to a temperate climate with four different seasons. Check individual growing directions of your herbs to determine how to support them.

The purpose of late-season herb gardening is to wrap up the growing season and prepare for the dormant season. Bring in the final harvest, then prepare plants and ground for rest. Often this means resisting the temptation to meddle. It also makes this a poor time to start most projects, except for late-season ones or things that require a resting period.

Deadheading

Deadheading is the process of picking flower heads off the plant immediately after they finish blooming. Doing this maximizes the number of flowers produced. It is most important in the late season for extending the bloom season. Do this if you keep a show garden or cultivate edible flowers. Picking off flower buds as soon as they appear is something you start doing earlier if you want the leaves instead of the flowers, but you have to keep doing it until the plants dry out.

A related technique is for herbs like chamomile that are grown specifically for their flowers. Pick each flower at its peak when fully open, and then dry them on a screen. This has the same general effects as deadheading with regard to encouraging further blossoms. Some types of chamomile really boom in late summer to early fall, so stay on top of them.

However, deadheading costs you the seeds. A wildlife garden benefits from seeds, and some herbs—like purple echinacea—are prime seed-bearing plants that attract songbirds such as goldfinches. If you plan to save seeds, then you need to let some of them mature. For these goals, either avoid deadheading altogether or make sure you stop in late summer so the plants have time to set some seeds before they die or go dormant. I rarely deadhead anything, unless I am growing the flowers to eat, in which case harvesting them serves that purpose.

Seed Saving and Sowing

Many types of herbs reproduce with seeds, although some, like chives, are easier to propagate by dividing, as described later. For seeds, you will need to let at least some flowers mature. If they have pods, like morning glories, wait until the pods dry and turn brown. Some will actually open. You can then pick off the pods and gently crush them, then blow over the mass to remove the chaff. Other flowers, like marigolds, produce a bunch of seeds inside the old flower that you can simply pull off. Most mints have seeds that will sprinkle free if you hold out a tray and carefully shake the plant over it.

Because many seeds need to be chilled before they can sprout, you have two options for this. One is to sow them in autumn and let them overwinter naturally. This is the best bet with wildflower seeds; I just pick them and scratch them into the ground. I have blackberry lilies all over the place now. The other way is to store them indoors in a labeled envelope, then chill them right before you sow them in spring. This is a better option if you will need to start them early in flats indoors before transplanting outside. I also do this with some annuals, like morning glories and marigolds.

Final Harvest

The final harvest typically takes place sometime in fall. When that is depends on where you live, what you grow, and what this year's weather actually does. It's especially challenging in warm climates, where you may cut everything, only to find that some plants respawn a few weeks later due to vagaries in the weather. Harvesting is one of the more important tasks.

Annual plants may be harvested whole. You can pull them up or just cut them close to the ground. Some perennials, such as mint, also lend themselves to bunch harvesting as long as you don't uproot them. Simply grasp a bunch of stems in your hand and cut below there. I usually go out in fall and cut a whole lot of things all at once to dry in bunches.

Perennial plants often require more care. Some can be harvested by individual twigs, such as rosemary. Others need the leaves picked off, like sage. Take care not to damage the shape of woody herbs like these so you don't impair next year's growth. Soft-stemmed perennials like marjoram can be cut in bunches as described above. I rarely hand-pick leaves for mass preservation, just when I want to eat them.

Most late-season herbs are best preserved by drying. Individual flowers or leaves dry well on a screen. You can also use a food dehydrator if you have one. Bunches of herbs may be tied together at the base and hung to dry in a dark, airy place. If you have many herbs, you may want to invest in a drying rack that has multiple rungs to hold all your bunches.

Should you still have leafy summer herbs going, some of these preserve well by freezing. Herbs like basil can be cut whole and stuffed into a food processor. Chop them down and pack the mass into ice cube trays. If you're worried about freezer burn, pour olive oil into the cups to cover the leafy bits. Once frozen, pop out the herbal ice cubes and store them in a sealed bag.

Weeding, Trimming, and Pruning

Cleaning up the herb garden at the end of the growing season requires a considerable amount of weeding, trimming, and pruning. This leaves a tidy appearance for winter. It also reduces the chance of pests and certain diseases. However, it does destroy food and habitat for some beneficial species. Consider replacing that in a more convenient location or designating a wildlife corner that you don't tidy up. I tidy and mulch my bulb and herb beds, but not my wildlife gardens. The latter get cleaned up in spring, right before planting season.

First remove as many weeds as you can, green or brown. Take extra care to get the seeds. It is better to burn these if feasible. Home composting doesn't always reach high enough temperatures to kill weed seeds. I try hard to get garden weeds before they can drop seeds. This is a crucial task.

If you have tall, nonwoody plants that form stands, such as catmint, coneflowers, daylilies, or grass, then trim them back to about three inches above the ground. This makes it easier to cover the area with mulch and minimizes the risk of problems.

Woody plants need to be pruned with more care. Remove weak or broken branches, restoring the overall shape of the plant. This is important for brushy herbs such as rosemary, sage, and thyme. You should prune a flowering plant shortly after it stops blooming. That means prune your summer-flowering woody plants, such as gardenia and hydrangea, in late fall.

Autumn is also good for pruning things that flower on *new* growth, which will only emerge after the weather warms. Avoid pruning those that flower on the previous year's growth so you don't cut off the buds intended for spring. This is crucial with raspberries. Everbearing (a.k.a. fall-bearing) raspberries produce two crops and should be cut back in late fall after their second crop. They will send up new canes in spring. Summer-bearing raspberries flower on the previous fall's canes, and should be cut back immediately after their single summer crop. They will send up new canes not long after that, which mature by autumn. Conversely, if you want to kill woody weeds, cut them in fall and spot-spray the cut ends with herbicide. This kills most things. I do a lot of brush-clearing in fall after the leaves die, when it's cool and I can see what I'm doing.

Digging and Dividing

Some plants require a certain amount of disturbance in order to thrive. If you grow tender bulbs, you will need to dig them up before the frost arrives, clean off the dirt, and store them over the winter in a safe medium, such as damp sand, in a cool but not freezing place. Gladioli won't overwinter in cold climates.

Many bunching herbs, such as chives, need to be divided periodically. After their growth slows, dig them up. For small clumps, carefully pull them in half and replant them separately. Large clumps can be divided into more sections. If you look closely, you will see that each chive consists of a tiny bulb and a few round, narrow leaves; each one of those can actually form a clump, but it takes a long time. For a harvestable patch, you need at least a handful.

Running herbs, such as mint, also benefit from division. Look for the crowns amidst the runners. Dig up individual crowns and move them or give them away. If you can't identify crowns in a big patch, don't worry about it. Just use the blade of a shovel to dig up a large square, one shovel width per side, and move that. It should contain enough roots to restart.

Fertilizing

Some herbs are best fertilized in autumn. These include those most active in spring, such as saffron crocus or asparagus. It also includes anything you plant in fall, such as bulbs. The poorer your soil is, the more important your fertilizer is.

For new plantings, there are two good methods. One is to dig extra deep, put down fertilizer, cover with some dirt, then put in the plants, and finally cover with more dirt and a layer of mulch. The other is to plant normally, top with fertilizer, and cover with mulch. If you're dividing chives or other herbs, fertilizing in a ring several inches away from the plants will encourage them to spread. For these purposes, a balanced 10-10-10 fertilizer in slow-release pellets works well.

Also, examine your spreading plants. Do they have a ring of vibrant growth with an empty spot or lethargic stems in the middle? If so, they have depleted the nutrients they need in the center where they started growing. Refresh the area with some fertilizer. A good choice is seeding fertilizer, which has nutrients in crumbles of paper pulp. You can either sow new seeds yourself or let the surrounding plants self-seed into the favorable medium.

While you can apply composted manure at any time and in most places, autumn is the only time for applying raw manure on empty beds, because it will have all winter to break down. You can often obtain this for free just by offering to haul it yourself—messy, but frugal. If possible, get a mix of manure and soiled straw just as it gets forked out of the stalls, as this provides an excellent blend of "green" and "brown" materials. You can either till it into the soil, or spread it in a layer and top with soil or mulch. "Hot" manure such as sheep or poultry manure will also keep a bed warmer than usual, which is great for marginally hardy bulbs or around rose cones. The first greenhouses were sometimes heated by beds of decomposing manure, which is an option if you can't afford electric heat. Just keep the heating beds below the tables where the edible herbs grow, and you can have fresh hardy herbs through much of the winter.

Mulching

Mulch protects hibernating plants from the cold, dry weather of winter. It also conserves moisture and cuts down on competition from weeds. A dark mulch will absorb more sunlight and thus warm the ground faster. As an environmental aid, it provides shelter for overwintering wildlife, such as ladybugs. The materials and application differ depending on the type of plant and your goals. The harsher your winter is, the more important your mulch is.

Empty beds, or those with underground plants such as chives or other bulbs, can be covered with a thick layer of fallen leaves or bark chips. Watch for the first shoots to emerge in spring. Then rake off most or all of the mulch. You can usually reuse the mulch by piling it around herbal shrubs or other plants.

If you have roses, it gets a little more complicated. First cover the crown with dirt, then pile leaves over the rest, or put a little mulch over the crown and top with styrofoam or vinyl rose cones. The same approach works with many woody herbs, such as sage or rosemary.

For some plants, such as fruit trees and herbal shrubs, the best fertilizer and mulch come from fallen leaves. Gather autumn leaves as they fall. If you do not have many leaves, ask your neighbors; someone will probably be delighted to get rid of theirs. When possible, run the leaves through a shredder. Pile them in a compost bin or just a corner. Let them break down over the winter. You can toss them periodically if you wish—and if they aren't frozen into a solid mass—but you don't have to. In spring, spread a layer of partially composted leaves around your trees and bushes, a few inches away from the trunk.

Making Wildlife Shelters and Feeders

As you clean up your herb garden, consider wildlife. Some cleaning is necessary, but this often destroys food and habitat. Use some of the leavings to create wildlife shelters and feeders in a convenient place. The more you rely on permaculture, biodynamics, or other natural pest control in your herb garden, the more important it is to support animal helpers.

Small logs, loose bark, and fallen leaves can be piled together as shelter for beneficial insects, birds, and small animals. A deep pile of leaves or other mulch makes a good hibernating place for amphibians such as toads, who devour pests. Choose a protected place for your shelter, preferably with a southern exposure. A dark, flat rock provides a basking spot for cold-blooded critters to warm up.

If you have picked up pinecones or branches with shaggy bark, these make excellent feeders. Spread them with peanut butter or suet and then roll them in birdseed. Tie a string to one end and hang from a tree. Alternatively, a thistle feeder will replace flower seeds if you have deadheaded or harvested most of yours.

Some people like to hang feeders over an empty or dormant herb bed. Birds will scratch for seeds, which includes eating weed seeds, and deposit manure. Just make sure you use sterilized "no sprout" birdseed so you don't get volunteer sunflowers and such.

———

These are examples of the most common tasks for late-season herb gardening. Think about where you live, what you grow, and what the winter typically brings. Then decide on a list of "need to do" and "want to do" activities. Check them off as you go along. Now your garden will be ready for the dormant season!

The Miracle of Soil- and Water-Cleaning Plants

❦ Diana Rajchel ❦

It doesn't matter whether you live in a city or in the country—when you live in the industrial world, soil and water pollution can and will affect you. Heavy metals build up fast from bad disposal practices in mining, farming, and waste disposal. While in small doses, most substances remain harmless, the buildup from improper removal of waste can cause issues with everything from food safety to skin contact. Too often, this pollution infects low-income neighborhoods, whose residents don't always have the funds to relocate, but really, this spoilation can happen anywhere. For example, higher-income planned neighborhoods built on old landfills

often test high for soil contamination—and the land requires the same rehabilitation.

In the worst cases, environmental protection agencies may declare a patch of land a **brownfield**. This designation means that the earth itself has gathered so much poison that it is considered unsafe for any use. However, new technologies and research into plants as old as time are showing us a slow path to recovering all that poisoned land. It has become successful enough that some real estate firms specialize in the recovery and resale of these brownfields.

To understand what the plants do, it helps to understand what happens when someone dumps metals and petroleum into the ground. Soil catches all sorts of nasty things from our environment. Most concerning is when the dirt begins to fill with metals from the dumped chemicals. Over time, especially if we routinely eat food from, drink water from, and play on that patch of poisoned soil, those poisons become a part of our bodies. Once that happens, removing those poisons ranges from tediously painful to impossible.

Recovering Land and Water

Fortunately, it is often possible to remove toxic buildup in the land. Through **phytoremediation**—using plants for soil recovery—we can now remove toxic metals from the earth. These plants extract specific toxins from the dirt over time. The plants can then be harvested and burned, carbonizing them and concentrating the metals. While trace amounts of the poisons may remain in the ash, the transmutation itself reduces the need to find methods of disposal. In some cases, the ash can be tilled back into the soil and a second season of plants can even further reduce the problem chemicals.

Water sources can be recovered in similar ways. Certain plants that grow in rivers and ponds can suck poisons out of both the soil and the fluid. This process is called **phytoextraction**. Plants that do this absorb minerals, metals, and flotsam from bodies of water into their leaf structures.

In most cases, the metals remain within the plant. To remove the metals from the environment, the plants are carbonized (burned). However, some plants allow us to skip that step—through **phytovolatilization**, certain plants absorb metals from the soil and release them into the atmosphere. Alternately, certain plants with root systems located in water perform **phytofiltration**, when the roots of plants absorb pollutants from streams.

The limitation of phytoremedial and phytoextractive plants is that they can only recover soil or water as far as their roots reach. If you really want to restore a landfill, you probably need to plant specific trees. If you're just trying to get something nasty from roadside dumping out of your yard, dandelions may work just fine.

If you want to know what's happening with the water you use, the Environmental Working Group has an online tap water database. This search can tell you what's going on in your soil. It can also help you identify exactly what extraction plants you need.

If you're impatient, you may want to explore other methods of cleanup. But if you have the time, these plants can clean up and reclaim soil, water, and air over the course of a few years.

You may want to test your soil and water, then check your planting zone to see what plants work best on your property for environmental reclamation. While state agencies and home soil-testing kits can show you pH imbalances, you will need a private laboratory to give you any rundown on soil pollutants. You can find these laboratories with a web search. "Soil testing lab for home gardeners" renders the best results.

Recommended Plants

This list can give you a good idea of what plants may work best based on what you find in your soil and water. Look for plants that can grow happily in your zone and that remove the nasties that you want taken out. Just remember, especially if you grow any extractive fruits or vegetables—don't eat them! The plants that take the nastiness out of the soil *do* take it into themselves.

Amaranth

This flowering plant can absorb multiple metals at a high capacity. It has been tested as able to absorb lead, cadmium, nickel, and copper.

Bamboo

Bamboo grows fast and spreads easily. It assists in air, soil, and water recovery. It is also a highly flexible crop that provides food, dry goods, and textiles.

Boxwood Family

This family of slow-growing evergreen trees can act as a long-term solution to soil recovery. A version now grows on six of the seven continents. In addition to lead and arsenic, these trees have the capacity to absorb cyanide.

Bellflower

This pretty violet flower has been useful in landfill recovery in North America. While limited by the depth of its roots, it seems capable of sucking quite the chemical mélange out of the ground.

Broccoli

If you hate eating broccoli, now you have a reason to grow it with an excuse not to eat it. This plant can remove zinc, cadmium, and lead from the soil.

Cabbage Family

For purposes of soil recovery, often gardeners choose the ornamental rather than edible cabbages. This plant family extracts significant amounts of lead. As a bonus, you can plant these between rows in your garden to reduce weed growth.

Carnations

Carnations are being used to remove cadmium from fields in China with great results. Research on what other substances carnations may remove is underway.

Chrysanthemums and Marigolds

Both flowers help in removing cadmium and lead from soil; while chrysanthemum can absorb more metals, marigold's deeper roots can pull more of the metals out of the soil and move them into different parts of the plant.

Euphorbia

This species, which includes poinsettias, is known as a **hyperaccumulator** of metals. It goes a long way in reclaiming land after industrial use.

Fruit Trees

Fruit trees, especially old fruit groves, pose an interesting issue for developers. Many of the original planters used petrochemicals and metal-based pesticides to get rid of pests. Yet the trees themselves are also the best at removing those very poisons from the soil—sometimes offering a yield of poisoned fruit. People looking to recover private land can often let the poisoned trees continue to grow. This can increase soil recovery. They simply can't use the remaining fruits for food. This includes the fruits of apples, pears, quinces, apricots, plums, cherries, peaches, raspberries, loquats, almonds, and roses.

Garlic

Garlic bulbs do a great deal to improve farming. Not only do they act as a natural insecticide if planted between rows, they also absorb dichlorophenol, a chemical often used in commercial insecticides.

Geranium

This common, easy-to-grow plant does a great job extracting cadmium, lead, and nickel.

Gerber Daisy

This modest flower, already known for improving indoor air quality, can also remove petroleum products from the soil.

Honeysuckle

Honeysuckle is sweet and pretty and can draw bees. It also helps correct excess salt in the soil. If ocean water has flooded an area, a trellis of this vine can help your soil recover.

Lobelia

This shrubby flowering perennial looks pretty—and its roots accumulate cadmium from soil with great efficiency.

Mustard

Members of the mustard family are hyperaccumulators. You name it, they suck that right out of the soil. Urban farming initiatives are now experimenting with using mustard for recovering entire swathes of land for farming because of its efficacy.

Poplar Trees

Poplars remove lead and petroleum from soil, making them excellent for soil recovery on dumping sites and near industrial zones.

Red Clover

This wild plant, common in the Midwest, is one of the rare nonmetal hyperaccumulators. It also absorbs high volumes of zinc from the soil.

Rice

Rice shoots can easily extract cadmium and arsenic from the soil.

Sunflowers

Sunflowers appear to have superpowers. Not only can they remove lead, copper, and zinc from soils, but they also have demonstrated an ability to extract radioactive metals, including uranium and cesium. They have been key in soil recovery after Chernobyl. If you use them for this, at the end of the growing season, you need to remove and burn the plant, including the roots. Start a new crop the next year. Do not eat these sunflower seeds!

Vetiver

This fragrant grass is popular in water recovery. It sucks up lead and zinc especially, and something about it makes normally unbiodegradable metals somewhat more amenable to breakdown. Most members of the grass family can gather up toxins from the soil, but some may be limited by shallow roots.

Violets and Pansies

This lovely plant family can get most metals out of soil. They especially do well with the removal of lead and cadmium.

Wheat, Corn, and Barley

The long history of crop rotation has a new chapter in the face of soil recovery technology. Barley is known as a hyperaccumulator of aluminum, wheat removes lead from soil, and corn can absorb both lead and cadmium.

Willow

Once a popular headache medicine, the willow tree can resolve significant headaches of an environmental nature. It is a magnificent hyperaccumulator and can suck up mercury, petroleum, uranium, zinc, silver, chromium, cadmium, and much more. Since willows thrive on the edge of fresh bodies of water, they can serve in the recovery of both soil and water.

The list here is only a small sampling. At this time, over five hundred plant species are known to be useful in soil recovery, and more are being discovered. While not all plants can and do absorb pollutants, there are enough commonly available and easily cultivated that there's little reason not to try. The only caveats: don't eat them, and check first to make sure it's safe to burn them. If you have a yen for phytovolatilic plants, make sure you have someone that can test your air quality—breathing metals, even filtered through plants, can have a negative health impact. You can even create beautiful, decorative flower beds, thus beautifying and cleansing your environment!

Resources

Abdullah, Waddah Salman, and S. M. Sarem. "The Potential of Chrysanthemum and Pelargonium for Phytoextraction of Lead-Contaminated Soils." *Jordan Journal of Civil Engineering* 4, no. 4 (2010): 409–16. https://pdfs.semanticscholar.org/f45d/087e9371679e9044508ef5a0a9e67cd1fe76.pdf.

Camp, Zoe. "Get the Lead Out: How to Test Your Soil for Contaminants." *Garden Collage*, April 10, 2015. https://gardencollage.com/wander/gardens-parks/get-the-lead-out-how-to-test-your-soil-for-contaminants/.

"Carnation Cultivation to Tackle Soil Pollution." University of Wolverhampton. July 28, 2017. https://www.wlv.ac.uk/news-and-events/latest-news/2017/july-2017/carnation-cultivation-to-tackle-soil-pollution.php.

Encyclopedia.com. "Phytoremediation." Carol Steinfeld. Last modified August 3, 2019. https://www.encyclopedia.com/environment/encyclopedias-almanacs-transcripts-and-maps/phytoremediation.

Hemingway, Monica. "State-by-State List of Soil Testing Labs at Cooperative Extension Offices." https://gardeningproductsreview.com/state-by-state-list-soil-testing-labs-cooperative-extension-offices/.

Lorestani, Bahareh, Merhdad Cheraghi, and Nafiseh Yousefi. "The Potential of Phytoremediation Using Hyperaccumulator Plants: A Case Study at a Lead-Zinc Mine Site." *International Journal of Phytoremediation* 14, no. 8 (September 2012): 786–95. doi: 10.1080/15226514.2011.619594.

Mahdieh, Majid, Mojtaba Yazdani, and Shahla Mahdieh. "The High Potential of *Pelargonium roseum* Plant for Phytoremediation of Heavy Metals." *Environmental Monitoring and Assessment* 185, no. 9 (2013): 7877–81. doi:10.1007/s10661-013-3141-3.

Murakami, Masahiko, Noriharu Ae, and Shizuko Ishikawa. "Phytoextraction of Cadmium by Rice (*Oryza sativa* L.), Soybean (*Glycine max* (L.) Merr.), and Maize (*Zea mays* L.)." *Environmental Pollution* 145, no. 1 (2007): 96–103. doi:10.1016/j.envpol.2006.03.038.

Peng, Kefang, C. L. Luo, Yan Hui Chen, Guang Peng Wang, Xiang-Dong Li, and Zhen-guo Shen. "Cadmium and Other Metal Uptake by *Lobelia chinensis* and *Solanum nigrum* from Contaminated Soils." *Bulletin of Environmental Contamination and Toxicology* 83 (2009): 260–64. doi:10.1007/s00128-009-9701-0.

Ramana, S., A. K. Biswas Ajay, and Annangi Rao. "Phytoremediation of Cadmium Contaminated Soils by Marigold and Chrysanthemum." *National Academy Sciences Letters* 32, no. 11 (2009): 333–36. doi:10.1007/s11356-019-07256-7.

Trueman, Shanon. "Phytoremediation: Cleaning the Soil with Flowers." ThoughtCo. May 30, 2019. https://www.thoughtco.com/phytoremediation-cleaning-the-soil-with-flowers-419222.

Ziarati, Parisa, and Somaye Aledini. "The Phytoremediation Technique of Cleaning up Contaminated Soil." *Journal of Analytical and Environmental Toxicology* 4, no. 208 (2014). doi:10.4172/2161-0525.1000208.

"Viola walteri 'Blue Gem'." New Moon Nursery. http://www.newmoonnursery.com/plant/Viola-walteri-Silver-Gem (page defunct).

Ghastly Greens, Pernicious Plants, and Other Horrific Horticulture

⁂ Charlie Rainbow Wolf ⁂

You've no doubt heard the adage "All that glitters is not gold." In the garden, that could be altered to read "All that flowers is not food"! There are many culinary delights out in the wild, even in the hedgerows and ditches of the urban sprawl, but not everything that looks like it would be a delicious treat is tasty—or even safe!

Scandalous plants have peppered both history and literature throughout the ages. The philosopher Socrates died by drinking poison hemlock (*Conium maculatum*). It was a toxic plant that killed Abraham Lincoln's mother. She died of milk sickness, a severe and in this case fatal disease that she contracted from drinking the milk or eating the meat from a cow who had dined on the poisonous white snakeroot plant (*Ageratina altissima*). Computer scientist Alan Turing supposedly took his life by cyanide. Cyanide is a chemical found occurring naturally in some foods, such as beans and the seeds of apricots, peaches, and apples. In high enough quantities, these can be fatal (which is why as a young girl I was mortified to learn that my aunt ate apple cores with the seeds in them—but she lived to a ripe old age). Even today, the nicotine that occurs naturally in the tobacco plant has claimed millions of lives!

Plants don't have to be eaten or even touched to be hazardous, though. Who hasn't been fascinated by the venus flytrap (*Dionaea muscipula*) or perhaps the pitcher plant (*Sarracenia alata*), trapping their struggling prey and dining on the decomposing flesh? *Caulerpa taxifolia* might look lovely in your aquarium as a decorative algae, but it's one of the most invasive species in the wild, strangling out the indigenous wildlife. Other algaes, such as *Alexandrium fundyense* and *Alexandrium monilatum,* are responsible for the dangerous red tides that occur along the shorelines, creating harmful environments for both wildlife and humans.

There's no need to be frightened of Mother Nature. Educate yourself, and you will know what you can eat and what to avoid, what might be harmful if touched, and what can help should you inadvertently come into contact with them. This applies not just to greenery growing in meadows and forests; it also applies to innocent-looking items you might grow in your garden or the houseplants sitting on your windowsill. The list of harmful—and helpful—plants is ever evolving, for that is the way of the universe.

Beastly Berries

Holly

Many people decorate with holly both inside and outdoors. Its bright red berries stand out against the evergreen leaves and bring a touch of color to the cold winter days. However, holly berries contain a long list of poisons, including caffeine (which is actually an unregulated psychoactive drug that works on the central nervous system) and theobromine, potentially highly toxic to both pets and children.

The leaves of the holly plant (family Aquifoliaceae) warn you of its impending danger. They are sharp and, if eaten, can cause nausea, vomiting, and other intestinal problems. The most popular exception to this is *Ilex paraguariensis*, from which we get yerba mate tea.

Mistletoe

This is another favored seasonal decoration with a lot of legend and myth behind it. It's not native to the United States but can be seen growing wild in many parts of the world. It's known as "the kissing berry" because if a young girl refused the kiss, then marriage proposals would not occur during the coming year.

The pearl-white berries of the mistletoe look innocent and pretty. After all, this foliage is associated with kissing, so how harmful can it be, right? Wrong! The berries of the plant are highly toxic, and tyramine in *Viscum album*, while not usually fatal, causes nausea and vomiting and, in more serious cases, even seizures or cardiac arrest. Kiss under it, by all means, but don't let the berries anywhere near your lips!

Pokeweed

Elvis fans will remember him singing about "Poke Salad Annie." Poke salad—or sallet, as they say where we live—isn't actually a salad at all. It's the thrice boiled leaves of the young plant. If you've cooked the leaves and there's still a green hue to the water, you haven't done it right.

Poke (*Phytolacca americana*) has to have everything boiled out of it to make it edible because it is highly poisonous. Those who are sensitive to contact irritants may develop rashes and other skin problems even just touching poke. The roots and berries can be fatal if ingested. Why, then, have the leaves become such a legendary food source? Because not so very long ago, food was scarce, and poke was plentiful.

Toxic Trees

Laburnum

We had a lovely golden chain tree in our garden when we lived on a Lincolnshire farm and never thought anything of it. However, the elegant yellow flowers that draped gracefully over the lilacs against the church wall had quite a hidden secret: all parts of the tree are poisonous!

Laburnum anagyroides—the common laburnum—is native to Europe. The main toxin is cytisine, which when ingested can cause drowsiness, convulsions, frothing at the mouth, and more. It's not usually fatal, but it is extremely unpleasant, so let the seed pods be food for the eyes, not the stomach!

Sassafras

Sassafras albidum is indigenous to North America and highly prized for adding the taste and aroma to American root beer and sassafras tea. For that reason alone it has quite a cultural significance, but it also has been used in folk medicine and as a commodity for trade.

As innocent as soda pop and tea might sound, sassafras does contain safrole, which is closely monitored by the FDA. As well as having a negative effect on the nervous system, safrole is also labeled as a carcinogenic. You would have had to drink a *lot* of traditional root beer to feel the effects, but it is still considered scary enough for safrole to be banned as a food additive.

Yew

I was an avid bell ringer when I lived in the United Kingdom, and it seemed every churchyard sported an old yew tree. Yew (*Taxus baccata*) is said to be the protector of the dead, but there's a more practical side to this. Yew is not appealing to wildlife or farm animals, and, thus, planting yew trees next to the corpses in the churchyard helped ensure that the dead stayed buried!

Nearly every part of the yew tree contains cardiotoxins that are very poisonous to humans. Ingestion causes nausea, vomiting, convulsions, circulatory issues, and possibly heart attacks. Even the pollen of the yew can trigger lethargy, skin rashes, headaches, and asthma. The only part of the yew that is not harmful is the flesh of the berries—but the skin and the seeds are harmful, so why even bother?!

Vicious Vines

Clematis

Innocent and pretty, yes? False! These beautiful climbers are related to the buttercup family, and—believe it or not—they all hide a dark secret. The entire genus contains essential oils bonded to glycosides, and when these are ingested in large enough quantities, they can induce drooling, vomiting, and internal bleeding.

There are hundreds of varieties of clematis, some more irritating to the skin than others. Fortunately, the plant tends to taste very bitter, which deters inquiring minds from consuming it. Clematis is also used in herbal medicine, but as there are so many cultivars, it's best to leave that to the professionals.

Kudzu

Kudzu might not actually be considered toxic, but it's certainly thought to be noxious by those who are battling with it. To hear about its assets, you'd think that this fast-growing plant would be the answer to so many problems. It has value in the textile industry, for fuel, as food, and in herbal medicine. The problem with kudzu is that it is not native to the United States, and it's been labeled an invasive species.

The term *kudzu* refers to several varieties of plants in the genus *Pueraria* in the pea family. As naturalist Bill Finch writes, it isn't as invasive as the media would have you believe. It does contain many isoflavones, though, and for those who have a sensitivity to these substances, they may cause headaches, fevers, and stomach upsets when ingested, as well as contact rashes on the skin.

Poison Ivy

This is probably a no-brainer! Nearly everyone who has been caught with their hands in this prolific climber will remember this as something to avoid in the future. *Toxicodendron radicans* grows prolifically throughout eastern North America as well as parts of Asia. Even though it behaves similarly to ivy with its climbing habit, it's not actually an ivy. It's more closely related to pistachios and cashews!

Out west, it's *Toxicodendron rydbergii* to watch out for. The plants are related and likewise contain the same irritant, urushiol—which is found in the sap. Both *T. radicans* and *T. rydbergii* are unwelcome weeds in the garden, and handling them tends to cause a weepy and itchy rash in most people who touch it. It does have some value, though: its autumn colors are pretty, and it's a valuable food supply for wildlife.

Wicked Weeds

Giant Hogweed

Heracleum mantegazzianum might look like Queen Anne's lace (*Daucus carota*) initially, but please, please don't confuse the two! Queen Anne's lace has different leaves and is edible. Giant hogweed is much larger than Queen Anne's lace and is harmful to the touch.

The problem with giant hogweed is the sap. It is phototoxic, meaning it will make the skin sensitive to light, causing skin blisters and scarring. Furanocoumarin is found in every part of the plant, so avoid it at all costs. The side effects of the photodermatitis can be incredibly painful and long lasting. Don't try to deal with this plant on your own; contact a professional.

Jimsonweed

This is also known as the devil's snare, and that describes it very well! It's a toxic plant that gained notoriety as a mind-altering substance used in neoshaman magic. The reason that it induces the hallucinations is because ingesting it is deadly!

All parts of *Datura stramonium* are toxic and should never be handled by someone who is uneducated about this plant and its qualities. Even the smallest dose can be fatal. It's tempting to chase the high, but the accompanying urinary complications, hypothermia, amnesia, tachycardia, delirium, paranoia, and painful photosensitivity—which can last for up to a fortnight—make this one to stay away from.

Stinging Nettle

Its common name should be warning enough! Although native to Europe, the common nettle (*Urtica dioica*) is prolific throughout most of the world and comprises six subspecies, five of which can cause nasty contact dermatitis when touched. This is because of trichomes on the leaves and stems, which act like tiny needles injecting histamine into the skin.

When we lived on the farm, I noticed that near every patch of stinging nettles there was also a patch of dock growing. Crushed dock leaves (genus *Rumex*) are cooling and soothing to the skin that has been stung. There may be natural antihistamines in the dock, but at the time of writing this has not yet been determined.

Fatal Flowers

Foxglove

In *Flower Fairies of the Summer*, Cicely Mary Barker depicts the foxglove fairy beckoning the bumble bee to come and delight in the nectar of the beautiful blooms.

These woodland forest flowers are not as innocent as they seem. All parts of the plant have the potential to be deadly. Foxgloves are members of the genus *Digitalis*, and this is where the heart medicine digitalin originates. It's been used in the treatment of heart arrhythmia since 1775. Fatalities are rare, but they do exist. It's best to give this highly valued medicinal herb its due respect and steer children and animals well away from the enticing glove-like blossoms.

Foxglove's name comes from Old English foxes glofa (literally, "fox's glove"), but the connection between the flower and foxes remains elusive, according to etymologist Anatoly Liberman.

Hydrangea

What could be more serene than the pink, white, and blue hues of the common hydrangea bushes that you may have had in your garden as a child? Think again! The genus *Hydrangea* consists of more than seventy species, most of which are shrubs and bushes.

Hydrangeas pose more of a threat to dogs, cats, and horses than they do to people. All parts of the plant are toxic due to the presence of cyanogenic glycosides. You'd have to eat a lot of hydrangeas to poison yourself, but do watch for signs of diarrhea, vomiting, or personality changes in animals, and if you think that your beloved pet may have ingested something, seek the advice of your veterinarian.

Rhododendron

As a young Lincolnshire farmer's wife, I made the journey to Belvoir Castle every spring to marvel at the beautiful bold colors of the rhododendrons that grew on the grounds and in the surrounding woodlands. The beauty is deceptive. All parts of the plant are toxic to animals and humans.

Most of the danger comes from the evergreen leaves, because they might be mistaken as food in winter when sustenance is scarce. Signs of poisoning include vomiting and diarrhea, depression and weakness, and heart arrhythmia. Emma Bryce of *Modern Farmer* warns that even ingesting honey made from the nectar of the rhododendron flowers could cause health problems!

Horrible House Plants

Dumb Cane

This is one of the more popular houseplants, but it must be treated with caution. The ornamental leaves of *Dieffenbachia* are very pretty, but they should be kept away from animals and children. Ingesting them will produce undesirable reactions. Typical signs of *Dieffenbachia* toxicity include an unpleasant tingling or burning sensation of the lips and mouth. Drooling and swelling are not uncommon. This is rarely fatal and can usually be treated with analgesics and antihistamines.

Hyacinth

Nothing says "spring is coming" quite like the hyacinths peeking their heads up in the garden or even from the forced bulbs that grow in containers in late winter. The fragrant blossoms are colorful and delightful, but the bulbs are quite toxic. They contain significant amounts of oxalic acid and should be handled with gloves to prevent skin irritation.

The biggest threat the hyacinth poses is when it is mistaken for a root vegetable (don't laugh—I've known it to happen). The confusion comes from some members of the Scilloideae family with the common name of hyacinth not being true *Hyacinthus*—they're actually edible. *Leopoldia comosa*, often referred to as a tasseled grape hyacinth, is used in Mediterranean cooking and looks very similar to a grape hyacinth, but it is a completely different genus.

Poinsettia

Potted poinsettias appear in most florists and garden centers over the Christmas period. They're very pretty with their red and green bracts and fit in with the yuletide color schemes beautifully. They also come with a warning.

The leaves of *Euphorbia pulcherrima* contain a mild toxin that is akin to a latex reaction, and if you get this in your eye, it could cause temporary blindness. The plant is falsely considered deadly because of a tale from 1919: a two-year-old child died near a poinsettia bush, and it was assumed that he ingested part of it, according to Snopes. Ingesting any part of the plant may cause stomach irritation such as vomiting or diarrhea in people and in animals, but it is not considered to be fatal.

Conclusion

On the coast of Northern England, there is a skeleton of an old lighthouse that stood proudly in the shipping channel. Once a year, to raise money for the lifeboat (the Royal National Lifeboat Institution is a charity; all equipment is donated and all the crews are volunteers), we would follow the tide out to the Wyre Light, then quickly make our way back again to a party on the beach. This was all done under the watchful eye of those who knew where the sandbars were and where the quicksand was and when the tide was going to turn. I would no more try to make that walk without their guidance than I would eat vegetation I couldn't identify. Nature—whether it is a tide or a stormcloud or an innocent-looking flower—needs to be respected.

Resources

Barker, Cecily Mary. *Flower Fairies of the Summer*. In *The Complete Book of the Flower Fairies*. London: Warne, 2002.

Bryce, Emma. "The Strange History of 'Mad Honey.'" Modern Farmer. September 4, 2014. https://modernfarmer.com /2014/09/strange-history-hallucinogenic-mad-honey/.

Encyclopedia.com. "Digitalis." Larry Blaser. December 30, 2019. www.encyclopedia.com/medicine/drugs/pharmacology /digitalis.

Finch, Bill. "The True Story of Kudzu, the Vine That Never Truly Ate the South." *Smithsonian Magazine*, September 1, 2015. https:// www.smithsonianmag.com/science-nature/true-story-kudzu -vine-ate-south-180956325/.

Liberman, Anatoly. "Etymologists at War with a Flower: Foxglove." *OUPblog*, November 10, 2010. https://web.archive.org/web /20130508161659/http://blog.oup.com/2010/11/foxglove/.

Mikkelson, David. "Poisonous Poinsettias." Snopes. Accessed January 29, 2020. https://www.snopes.com/fact-check/poinsetting-it -out/.

Further Reading

Nelson, Lewis S., Richard D. Shih, and Michael J. Balick *Handbook of Poisonous and Injurious Plants*. 2nd ed. Berlin: Springer, 2007.

Scott, Timothy Lee. *Invasive Plant Medicine: The Ecological Benefits and Healing Abilities of Invasives*. Rochester, VT: Healing Arts Press, 2010.

Stewart, Amy. *Wicked Plants: The Weed That Killed Lincoln's Mother & Other Botanical Atrocities*. Chapel Hill, NC: Algonquin Books of Chapel Hill, 2009.

Your Garden,
the Day before Vesuvius

⌘ Thea Fiore-Bloom ⌘

Imagine you're a noblewoman in ancient Rome. Life's been good to you, and like most of your 1-percent, patrician pals, you have a palace in the city and a villa in Pompeii on the coast. It's a bright fall morning on October 23, 79 CE.

Which, unfortunately, happens to be the day before Vesuvius will crack open, its pyroclastic flow sluicing down the mountain and preserving your Pompeiian villa garden like a mollusk in the amber of time.

You innocently step out for what will be your last unhurried stroll around your fountain-rich, walled paradise. A shaft of ornamental wheat tickles your calf as you walk by.

What other plants, flowers, and herbs do you see?

There are a few people alive today who might shock you with how well they know what is where in your ancient garden. People who could say that your pergola over there is most likely covered with grapevine, not roses. And that wheat shaft that just tickled your calf? It was black, not beige.

Who are these people? Have they taken one too many "Know Your Past Life" seminars?

Nope. Actually, they're mostly scientists, not psychics, working alongside fresco historians and other scholars—people like archeobotanists and environmental biologists armed with new plant-identifying capabilities.

For example, the pioneering study of previously ignored subterranean, carbonized root imprints by botanical archeologist Wilhelmina Feemster Jashemski has helped researchers better identify *what* species of plant were grown exactly *where* in the gardens of Pompeii.

Scholars, garden directors, and museum heads have not only studied these ancient gardens, they've also re-created them. This is wonderful news because now you and I can enjoy stepping back in time into a Roman garden, the day before Vesuvius—without fear that we too will be preserved like a mollusk in amber.

Villa dei Papiri, from the Ashes

Horticulturist Michael D. DeHart (Supervisor for Grounds and Gardens for the J. Paul Getty Trust) has devoted the last twenty years of his life making it his business to give visitors to the Getty Villa Museum in Malibu the pleasure of walking in gardens similar to those that used to flourish at the ancient Villa dei Papiri in Herculaneum (also tragically buried by Vesuvius).

The Getty Villa garden is a great example of archeological garden reconstruction and has been lauded for being one of the best gardens created in the twentieth century. DeHart was kind enough to give me a walk around its vast herb garden to help me see the plants there through more . . . Roman eyes, eyes that seem to have connected all elements of nature (from a rustling leaf to a clap of thunder) with a goddess or god. Let's look at a sample of eight must-have trees, herbs, and flowers Pompeiians prized in their gardens and get tips from DeHart on how to grow them at home.

Two Sacred Trees to Grace Your Entry

When you enter or exit many of the long rectangular gardens at the Getty Villa you often will pass between carefully selected pairs of trees. Getty author Jeanne D'Andrea notes that an entire carbonized bay laurel tree was dug up in the outer peristyle of the House of the Faun in Pompeii, so we'll begin with bay (1982, 37).

Grecian Bay Laurel, *Laurus nobilis*

To a Roman, a branch of bay laurel smelled like victory. Roman heroes donned bay wreaths at games and festivals. Apparently, Julius Caesar almost constantly wore a laurel wreath in public, to the great annoyance of his critics, who viewed this as a pompous display of hubris. But, according to D'Andrea, Caesar's defenders claimed Julius sported his laurels not to boast of battle success, but to hide his big bald spot (1982, 35).

Romans also revered the bay laurel for its apotropaic properties. In other words, they believed it could ward off evil—evil in the form of curses, plague, and lightning strikes. And Pompeiians adored sculpting bay into topiary.

"The bay laurel is a tree that wants to be a shrub," said De-Hart. "It responds like crazy to pruning. The Romans shaped bay laurel into little umbrella domes, big mushroom domes, tall columns, and even high hedges." The Getty has a huge screen hedge of bay laurel at its entrance.

Bay can also do well in pots. You'll need a container twenty inches deep and wide. Make sure the loamy potting soil (ideally with compost added) can drain well before you transplant it. This plant is hardy to about 20 degrees.

Olive Tree, *Olea europaea*

Don't let your laurel get lonely. Bay laurel was sacred to Apollo, so maybe plant Minerva's favorite tree nearby, a tree whose leaves can shine silver in the sun: the olive.

The mythic founders of Rome (Romulus and Remus) were said to have been born under a mighty olive tree. And the twins might have died under that olive too, if it hadn't been for the she-wolf who raised them to manhood.

"We grow 'Swan Hill' olives here at the Getty Villa," said DeHart, "because they're fruitless. It prevents visitors from slipping and falling on them as they walk by." If you want fruit, DeHart recommends you go with basic *Olea europaea.* "But know it's a tremendous amount of work for a homeowner to produce edible olives. It's more brining and rinsing than you'd think to get just one olive to plunk in a martini."

Olive trees can be grown in pots on patios. In the beginning, the saplings need lots of water, but they can grow to be drought-tolerant if they're nurtured enough initially to establish complex root systems. Plant in full sun in dry, alkaline soil. This tree is hardy to about 20 degrees.

Two Holy Herbs

Let's leave our treed entrance behind and walk on the garden's central path toward its gurgling fountain and pool. On either side of this path lie symmetrical pairs of herb beds overflowing with sweet basil.

Sweet Basil, *Ocimum basilicum*

We see basil and think . . . *bruschetta.*

But Romans saw basil and probably thought *royalty.* The word *basil* comes from the Greek word *basilikon,* which means "kingly." "Basil was an imperial herb in antiquity," said De-Hart.

Romans may have revered basil, but apparently ancient Greeks had a complex relationship to it, because they believed in order to grow lush, ritually powerful basil, you needed to shout obscene curses at it as you planted it, writes D'Andrea (1982, 32).

When Greeks weren't cursing at their basil, they were using it for healing nasty bites. Pliny the Elder wrote in *Natural History* that to survive the bites of rabid dogs, poisonous snakes, and sea scorpions, one should administer a basil-infused tincture made of wine and vinegar (D'Andrea 1982, 32).

Basil will flourish in anything from partial shade to full sun in moist, well-drained soil. It can survive year-round in places where the temperature doesn't dip below about 35 degrees.

Mint, *Mentha* spp.

If you were going to attend a formal banquet in Pompeii this evening, you might stroll into your garden to gather mint for your wreath. Mint was fashionable headgear at banquets since the herb was thought to both stimulate the appetite and calm the emotions. In fact, mint was believed to be so calming Roman soldiers were forbidden to eat or wear the herb for fear it would do too good a job of tamping down aggression (D'Andrea 1982, 58).

"Mint was a major player in ancient meat sauces," said De-Hart, who recommends anyone interested in ancient lifestyles and cookery check out the work of Marcus Gavius Apicius. "Apicius was the Martha Stewart of the first century," said De-Hart. "According to Apicius, all meat sauces had oregano and mint in them (and practically every other herb in existence). There was no refrigeration then. Romans probably needed complex herb sauces to mask things going off," said DeHart.

But fish was a different story. If you wanted truly fresh fish, you need not have gone farther than your garden pool, which DeHart says was like a live fish refrigerator for some Romans. And those fish often benefited from the cool shelter that parasol-like water lilies provided there.

One Mythic Lily for
Your Central Reflecting Pool

Cleopatra's Blue Nile Water Lily, *Nymphaea* **spp.**

The scientific name for water lily is *Nymphaea*, coming from the Greek word for *nymph*. In myth, nymphs were semi-divine spirit beings that guarded springs, pools, and waterways.

"Cleopatra grew a gorgeous violet-blue–hued water lily species in ancient Egypt, which we grow here at the Getty Villa and think Romans too may have enjoyed in their pools," said DeHart.

"The colorful tropical varieties like the blue do not tolerate the cold winters of even warm regions like California and

If you had a moonlit, wine-fueled tryst for two in a quiet field in first-century Rome, the only thing you and your partner might be found wearing come morning were your myrtle crowns. Why myrtle? The plant was sacred to Myrtea, goddess of myrtle, who became known as Venus. Queen Victoria rocked a myrtle crown in her 1847 wedding portrait, and delicate myrtle tiaras crafted from silver filigree are still worn by brides today.

are replaced every spring," explained DeHart. (But apparently, there are a few hardier, simple-hued hybrid species you can grow that can last longer than one season, with proper care.)

Plant your blue water lily in full sun in a pond with rich humic soil. Top with an inch of sand to keep the roots in that humic layer. Hardiness depends on species.

One Divine Flower at the Fountain

Romans probably enjoyed flowers not only *in* their fountains but around them as well. And their favorite flower might have been the rose.

Damask Rose, *Rosa* 'Autumn Damask'

Imperial Rome was mad for roses. And the silky bomb of a flower was sacred to the divine trifecta of Venus, Bacchus, and Flora. Vast quantities of rose petals were strewn on banquet floors and used to make rosewater to bathe in. Roses were tossed on Roman roads prior to victory parades, their petals giving off a memorable scent when crushed under the wooden wheels of passing chariots (D'Andrea 1982, 72).

I'd never smelled a Damask rose before my day with De-Hart at the Getty. It's so deliciously complex, with a vanilla base note, a violet middle note, and a kind of cinnamony-lemon top note. I now understand why perfumers have secretly included it in cologne for centuries.

This complexly scented rose is simple to grow. "Damask roses are so easy to grow. They're on their own root; they aren't even grafted. It is such an original, unfettered, unhybridized rose—everyone should try growing them," said DeHart. Plant in full sun in fertile, moist, well-drained soil. Hardy to about -10 degrees.

If you keep walking beyond the fountain, you'll pass through another long set of symmetrical herb beds and pairs of fruit trees. Perhaps if this were your villa, you'd pick a few pomegranates, lemons, figs, or peaches before scooting under your grapevine-covered pergola to head back in for *ientaculum* (breakfast).

A Holy Roman Vine
for the Perimeter of Your Garden

'Rogers Red' Grape, Hybrid of *Vitis californica* and
V. vinifera 'Alicante Bouschet'

Vine-draped pergolas like those at the Getty Villa doubled as personal exercise paths in Pompeii. They often hugged along the interior walls of a garden and provided dappled shade. But grapes and grapevine were more than sources of wine and shade for Romans. They were symbols of the Roman god Bacchus, the master of revelry, fertility, and the theater arts.

The Getty's pergola is covered with a vine that produces a delicious purple cabernet grape popular in Sonoma called 'Roger's Red'. If you visit the Villa in autumn, you'll see 'Roger's Red' has leaves that flush a Pompeiian crimson before falling.

"You don't need a pergola, an arbor, or even any structure with a roof to grow your own grapes," said DeHart. "You just need a post, another post, and some wire strung in between. The post holds up the woody cane and the wire holds up the lightweight vine. You prune it back every winter. You could even set that up on a patio." Grapes need full sun and fertile, well-drained soil to thrive. The plants are hardy to about 10 degrees.

The Flower That Rambles the Ruins

Alyssum, *Lobularia maritima*

Until recently, I could never figure out why on some days when I walk the gardens at the Getty Villa I get instantly transported back to my visit to the ruins of Pompeii, but on other Getty walks, I don't.

I finally figured out it depends on whether or not the alyssum is in bloom. The ruins of Pompeii were carpeted with alyssum when I was there. It's a ground-hugging plant with tiny white flowers. Alyssum is easy to overlook, but it gives off a show-stopping scent reminiscent of neroli and honey.

To bring a bit of ancient Italy home with you, grow your own alyssum. Butterflies love it. Plant it months before the first frost. Just generously sprinkle the seed of the white, pink, or purple variety on top of turned soil and gently press in. You want the seeds close together so that you can recreate the scattered, wild, white carpet effect you may have seen, or will one day see, on a visit to Pompeii. Make sure to water alyssum daily in hot weather.

A Virtual Visit

For photos of Pompeiian gardens that have been brought back to life in Italy, visit Cher Stone Beall's blog post "Gardens of Pompeii as a Roman Legacy" at www.electrummagazine .com/2015/12/the-gardens-of-pompeii-as-a-roman-legacy/. The Getty Villa website shows tantalizing snippets of their Roman gardens at www.getty.edu/visit/villa/.

Resources

Bowe, Patrick, and Michael D. DeHart. *Gardens and Plants of the Getty Villa.* Malibu, CA: J Paul Getty Museum, 2011.

D'Andrea, Jeanne. *Ancient Herbs in the J. Paul Getty Museum Gardens.* Illustrated by Martha Breen Bredemeyer. Los Angeles, CA: J. Paul Getty Museum, 1982.

DeHart, Michael D. Personal interview by the author. Malibu, CA, 2019.

Giesecke, Annette. *The Mythology of Plants: Botanical Lore from Ancient Greece and Rome.* Los Angeles, CA: J Paul Getty Museum, 2014.

Jashemski, Wilhelmina Feemster. *A Pompeian Herbal: Ancient and Modern Medicinal Plants.* Austin: University of Texas Press, 1999.

An Herb Gardener's Journal:
A Sundial of the Year

≫ James Kambos ≪

My herb garden slopes down away from my house. I can see it from where I write. As I look at my herb garden, I feel that it's sort of a sundial of the year. What I mean is that whenever I gaze out at it, I can tell what season it is. Right now the goldfinches are riding the seed heads of the zinnias, and the tall joe-pye weed is swaying in the breeze. So, I know it's summer. Then when I see the soft silvery lamb's ears surrounded by fallen rusty sere leaves, I know it's autumn. When I see the sharp edges and contours of the herb garden's border and can clearly see the herb garden's statues, then I know winter is in charge. Finally, when the gray-brown landscape is punctuated

by clumps of delicate white snowdrops blooming, I know the wheel of the year has turned toward spring.

As herb gardeners, we're so lucky. Our lives are enriched by this sundial of the year. In every season the scents, textures, colors, and tastes that come from the herb garden change and bring much joy to our lives. Whether your herb garden consists of a few potted herbs on a patio, a couple of raised beds, or an elegant formal herb garden surrounded by boxwood shrubs, an herb garden presents a different picture and has different needs each season.

Our activities as herb gardeners change too as the seasons turn. Planting, hoeing, harvesting, and planning are governed by the sundial of the year.

What I've done here is put together a brief journal of what I do during each season of the year in my herb garden. My garden is located in Ohio in zone 6. You can tweak my suggestions to suit your area (see page 218). Keep in mind the seasons may arrive a little earlier or later each year, so adjust for that too.

I'm no botanist. I'm just a guy who inherited a love of herb gardening from his grandparents. This is just what I do each season, and my herb garden has rewarded me with joy and beauty for many years.

I'll begin my journal, or sundial of the year, with spring, when the gardening season begins.

Spring: The Renewal

The air is still cool, but the sun begins to warm the soil. The frost rises from the earth. You can smell the renewed soil. It has a damp earthy scent. I take a deep breath and fill my lungs with its woodsy fragrance. My hands ache to feel the soil, but first I must tend to spring chores.

The first spring job in the herb garden is weeding. If you don't do it now, you'll pay for it later. To do this I rely on a good long-handled hoe. I start at one end of the garden and loosen and then remove any weeds. As I remove them, I toss the weeds onto a grassy area. Next, if necessary, I weed again on my knees using a kneeling pad for garden use. For this close work, I also keep a pair of gloves handy as well as a short handheld hoe. When done, I rake up all the weeds I've left in the grass.

Don't toss pulled weeds into the compost pile, as they may take root again. Instead, leave them on the grass and go over them with your mower.

Weeding like this takes about two days. After the weeding, I give the entire garden a good top dressing of rich garden soil or compost. For this, I buy it bagged at a garden center. I spread it about one inch deep using a garden rake. Then for established herbs that like lime, such as thyme or lavender, I scratch a small amount of lime around their base.

If you're like me, you can't wait to plant something. Even though it's still cool, some herbs can be planted around mid-April. These include chives, parsley, and thyme.

Now, lean on your hoe. Watch your herb garden begin to turn green. Soon the sundial of the year tells us it's summer.

Summer: The Ripening

All the hard work you've done comes to fruition in the summer. Now the herb garden is at its peak; the ripening has begun. Oregano, basil, and mint, along with other herbs, are ready for harvesting. The day starts early for me and ends at dusk with a walk along the old fence where the bee balm blooms.

Summer tasks in the herb garden should be chores that promote the health of the garden.

Let's begin with watering. Water early in the morning. This prevents rapid moisture evaporation and allows the foliage to dry quickly, preventing disease. Water at the base of the herb plants. Avoid "top spraying," which allows moisture to stay on the leaves. This may cause mildew. During a dry spell, a good soaking once a week should do it.

Next, don't forget to mulch. A one-to-two-inch layer of mulch will lock in moisture and keep weeds down. Keep the mulch away from the base of herb plants. This prevents harmful insects from nesting too close. If you weeded well in the spring, weeds shouldn't be a big problem now. But as you see weeds, pull them. This improves appearances and helps air circulation.

To keep the herbs healthy, remember to always remove discolored foliage. If an entire herb plant looks wilted, remove the entire plant and throw it away. Also, don't plant herbs too closely. If you need to fill in a bare spot, fill it in with an annual herb, which should prevent overcrowding.

Harvest your herbs by cutting them on a dry sunny morning. This ensures peak flavor. Then rinse them in cool water and let them dry. Next, tie the herbs in bundles of about three stems. Hang the bundles away from direct sun to finish drying.

Above all, enjoy your herb garden. Don't forget to savor its scents, textures, and colors. Also, take time to visit a friend's herb garden. You'll return energized and with new ideas.

Mornings begin to turn cool and shadows fall differently. The sundial of the year says autumn has arrived.

Autumn: The Reaping

There's a special beauty to the herb garden in the autumn. The annual flowers and herbs have been frosted and been removed. Now the silver-hued herbs dominate—lamb's ear, southernwood, and sage are a few. How beautiful they look on a moonlit night!

Now is the time to reap. Harvest any herbs you still wish to cut and use for arrangements or for seasoning. But this also is a time to pause and reap the memories you've made from your herb garden. Remember all the joy your garden has brought you this year. Before autumn ends, walk among your herbs on a sunny afternoon. With each step the scents of the thyme, sage, and lavender rise into the air. With every scent you can relive summer.

But there's still work to do. Cutting back the leafy herbs is a personal preference. Doing it now, however, will save work come spring. Woody herbs such as lavender shouldn't be cut back.

Make sure none of the roots of your herbs are exposed. If you see any exposed roots, cover them with soil and tamp down with your foot. If roots are exposed during the coming winter, it can kill a plant.

Some folks like to add a fresh layer of mulch now to keep the herb garden looking tidy. If you do this, let the ground's surface freeze first. If you mulch before the ground freezes, small rodents such as field mice may move in beneath the mulch and cause damage.

Autumn is also a time to clean and store garden tools. I like to rub off any hardened dirt and then wipe the tool with a clean rag. Tools such as shears or clippers should be oiled. When the tools are clean, store them in a shed or garage to prevent rusting.

Keeping an herb garden journal is a great way to keep track of what worked and what didn't grow well in your herb garden. You can also include photos and sketches.

On autumn mornings frost sequins the grass. By dusk dry fallen leaves click as they blow through the herb garden. At night the wind moans as it rattles the storm door.

Now the sundial of the year warns us winter is coming, and it won't stop until it owns the land.

Winter: The Rest

The tools are in my shed, the basil and dill are drying in the kitchen, and the logs are crackling in my woodstove.

It's winter.

It's time for the herb garden, and the herb gardener, to rest. There's a special beauty to the herb garden in winter. The lines and contours of the garden are visible. Now I can see my statue of a boy holding a sheaf of grain watching over the side of the garden. It's dusted with snow.

Most herb garden activities take place indoors now. Planning, placing seed orders, and just dreaming about next year's garden are some of winter's pleasant herb garden tasks. However, there are a few ways to beautify the winter herb garden outside. During the winter and holiday season, the herb garden's appearance could be enhanced in a few simple ways. You could drape a pine garland along a fence. A pine and herb wreath on a garden gate or just a red bow on a shed door are a few ways to add charm to the winter herb garden.

In the winter you can still enjoy your herb garden inside your home too. Just cooking with all the herbs you've harvested will fill your home with great tastes and aromas. Get crafty and incorporate your dried herbal materials into homemade gifts and decorations.

I also encourage you to keep some graph paper on hand. Sketching your ideas for future herb beds is a pleasant activity for a winter day.

Bit by bit as winter progresses, I notice the hours of daylight lengthen. Soon after, I see the snow begin to thaw around the English thyme. The sundial of the year is giving me signs—spring is near.

The renewal of the earth has begun again.

Cooking

Growing Vegetable Soup:
The Story of My Soup Garden

⪢ Kathy Martin ⪡

There are lots of themes one can imagine for a garden—different color schemes, gardens celebrating different cultures, many varieties of one type of plant, formal or native gardens, and so on. As a volunteer garden steward at the Massachusetts Horticultural Gardens at Elm Bank, a project I had was to design and grow a display garden bed. I chose the theme of a soup garden.

To develop my garden plan, I chose my favorite soup recipes: tomato soup, potato and leek soup, butternut squash soup, spring snap pea soup, and mixed greens soup. I collected the recipes, listed out the ingredients, and drew up a plan.

I have often grown vegetable gardens by planting in random fashion in garden beds. It works. But for this display garden, I drew out a detailed plan. I have to admit I spent many pleasant hours on it during the cold months of the winter. Once I had my plant list, I wrote up the amount of space each plant required: tomatoes, eighteen inches; onions and leeks, four inches, etc. I drew up circles to scale and moved them around on my garden plan. (I used PowerPoint, but many other tools, including pencil and graph paper, work easily as well.) I also considered how long and when the plants would grow. Greens and peas grow in early spring and can be harvested, leaving room for the summer plants like tomatoes and squashes. So for some areas of my soup garden, I had a succession planting plan.

Soup is a wonderful way to enjoy herbs and vegetables at any time of the year. The soup garden plan I developed and grew is included on page 287. Be creative and put together a vegetable soup of your own invention.

The garden did very well that year. We had labels in the bed explaining the theme and listing the recipes. I grew a bumper crop of 'Sugar Daddy' snap peas, a lot of big fall leeks, and nice 'Waltham Butternut' squash. The vegetables we harvested went to local food pantries. I don't know if they ended up being used for soup. Maybe.

Vegetable Soups: Stocks and Herbs

Vegetable soup can be a very simple food. It's a staple and a hearty nutritious food. I can imagine the very earliest peoples with a kettle, vegetables, spices, and a broth. Not only can vegetable soup be simple, but it can also be complex, gourmet, or spicy . . . so many variations. For a cook to set out to make vegetable soup is like an artist with a canvas or a gardener with a new plot of soil. There are few combinations of herbs and vegetables that won't work to create a delicious soup.

Vegetable soup often refers to a soup made with a mix of many vegetables. A traditional American vegetable soup would include onions, carrots, celery, peas, and green beans. It might also include potatoes, cabbage, or tomatoes. It would use a vegetable or a chicken broth and would be flavored with thyme, garlic, salt, and black pepper. But take this simple recipe and change the spices, the vegetable combinations, and there is a world of soups.

Generally, a vegetable soup is based on a stock, usually beef, chicken, or vegetable. A stock is made by simmering meat scraps, bones, and/or vegetables in water for two to six hours. The stock is left unseasoned. Seasoning happens when the soup is being made. Often the type of seasoning one wants to use is the first selection in making a soup. Based on that, complementary meats, vegetables, and condiments are added.

Beef stock is a rich starting point for vegetable soup. It combines well with bold herbs and spices, such as chili peppers, oregano, basil, bay leaf, rosemary, and curry powder. Chicken stock can be delicate or robust. Combinations of onion, paprika, parsley, red pepper flakes, sesame seeds, or chives add nice flavor. Vegetable stock often has a tomato base. Herbs and spices that complement this are the classic Italian flavorings, oregano, parsley, garlic, onion, basil, and chives.

The herbs I grew in my soup garden were garlic, parsley, oregano, basil, chives, cayenne pepper, shallots, and mint. I didn't grow the bay leaf, black pepper, nutmeg, and curry powder that are in my recipes—they had to come from the store.

Recipes from My Soup Garden

For my demonstration soup garden, I used three classic American recipes: fresh tomato soup, leek and potato soup, and butternut squash soup. I added a couple more unusual recipes that make use of spring vegetables: snap pea soup and green soup. All of these are pureed soups, so an immersion blender is handy to have.

Fresh Tomato Soup

- 1 small onion, chopped
- 1 bay leaf
- 1 garlic clove, minced
- 2 pounds fresh peeled and seeded tomatoes (or a 28-ounce can of whole tomatoes)
- 1 slice bread, torn
- 1 cup vegetable or chicken broth
- 2 teaspoons total fresh oregano, basil, parsley, in any combination, chopped
- ⅛ teaspoon sea salt
- Freshly ground pepper to taste
- Fresh chives
- 2 tablespoons olive oil

Sauté the onion, bay leaf, and garlic in oil in a stock pot for about 3 minutes. Mash the tomatoes with a potato masher and add to the pot. Stir in the torn bread, broth, herbs, salt, and pepper. Bring the soup to a low simmer and cook for about 5 minutes. Remove the bay leaf and then blend the soup with an immersion blender. Serve the soup warm or piping hot topped with fresh chives and a drizzle of olive oil. Serves 3–4.

Leek and Potato Soup

>   3 tablespoons butter
>
>   2½ cups chopped leeks (2 small or 1 large). Use white and light green parts of the leek plus about 2 inches of the dark green part.
>
>   1 medium yellow onion, chopped
>
>   2 cups roughly chopped 'Yukon Gold' potatoes (3 medium potatoes)
>
>   1 cup chopped celeriac
>
>   1 quart light chicken broth
>
>   6 ounces plain yogurt or cream
>
>   Chives, thyme, parsley, or any combination of these, chopped
>
>   Salt
>
>   Black pepper

Melt the butter in a heavy soup pan and then add the leeks and onion. Sauté until golden (about 3 minutes). Add potatoes, celeriac, and broth and then cover and bring to a boil. Reduce the heat and simmer until the potatoes are soft (about 30 minutes). Roughly puree the soup in a food processor or with an immersion blender. Add the yogurt and whisk. Season with the herbs, and then add salt and pepper to taste. Serves 10.

Butternut Squash Soup

>   2 tablespoons butter
>
>   1 small onion, chopped
>
>   1 stalk celery, chopped

1 medium carrot, chopped

2 medium white or sweet potatoes, cubed

1 medium butternut squash (or other winter squash),
peeled, seeded, and cubed

1 quart chicken or vegetable stock

Salt to taste

Black pepper to taste

Ground cayenne pepper to taste

Dash of nutmeg and 1 teaspoon curry powder, or 2 teaspoons chopped fresh thyme and rosemary

Sour cream

Melt the butter in a heavy soup pan and cook the onion, celery, carrot, potatoes, and squash for 15 minutes or until golden
brown. Pour in enough of the stock to cover the vegetables.
Bring to a boil, and then reduce the heat and simmer for 40
minutes or until all vegetables are tender. Puree in a food
processor or with an immersion blender, adding extra stock
as needed. I like to leave the soup a bit chunky for a home-
style version. Season the soup with the herbs and spices, using
more or less to taste, and then serve with a dollop of sour
cream. Serves 8–10.

Snap Pea Soup with Mint and Lemon

1½ pounds snap peas, stems removed and rinsed

½ cup minced shallots

2½ cups chicken or vegetable broth

¼ cup grated parmesan

2 tablespoons chopped fresh mint

Zest of 1 lemon

2 tablespoons fresh lemon juice

½ teaspoon sea salt

Freshly ground pepper to taste

¼ cup crème fraiche (or heavy cream or yogurt)

Blanch the peas for about 5 minutes in a large pot of boiling water, and then drain and place in an ice bath. Sauté the shallots for about 3 minutes in a stock pot. Remove the pot from heat and add the peas, broth, parmesan, mint, lemon zest, lemon juice, salt, and pepper. Blend the soup using an immersion blender.

Reheat until just hot. Finish by whisking the crème fraiche into the pureed soup. When serving, top each bowl with a dollop of crème fraiche and a mint leaf. Serves 4–6.

Green Soup with Rice and Chickpeas

This soup looks and tastes very green. It includes a lot of greens. It's really nice with the brown rice and chickpeas added to the bowl before serving. This recipe was adapted from the blog *Cookie and Kate*.

2 large yellow onions, chopped

2 tablespoons extra-virgin olive oil, plus more for garnish

¼ teaspoon salt, plus ¾ teaspoon

3 cups water plus 2 tablespoons, divided

¼ cup rice, rinsed (I like a short-grain brown rice.)

About 1½ pounds (20 cups) mixed summer greens (e.g., Chinese broccoli, bok choy, broccoli rabe, kale, green chard, celery, and spinach), roughly chopped with ribs and tough stems removed

4 cups vegetable broth or a light chicken broth

Big pinch of cayenne pepper, to taste (¼ teaspoon or
  more)

1 tablespoon lemon juice, or more to taste

For serving:

  Cooked brown rice

  Warm chickpeas for serving

  Lemon wedges

  Freshly ground black pepper

Caramelize the onions in 2 tablespoons oil with ¼ teaspoon
salt in a large skillet over medium-high heat. Cook the rice in a
dutch oven in 3 cups of water brought to a boil and then simmer, covered, for 15 minutes. To the cooked rice, add the caramelized onions, greens, broth, ¾ teaspoon salt, and cayenne.
Bring soup to a simmer, cover, and cook, stirring occasionally,
until the greens are tender but still bright green (about 10 minutes). Puree the soup in the pot with an immersion blender
and then stir in the lemon juice. Taste and add more lemon
juice, salt, or cayenne pepper as desired. Serve the soup over
cooked rice and chickpeas, garnish with a swirl of olive oil,
and serve with lemon wedges and freshly ground black pepper. Serves 8.

Vegetable Soups from Different Countries

There are some classic vegetable soups that are central to different cuisines around the world. Often these soups celebrate
a single vegetable that is central to a region, and the soup is
created with the seasonings, herbs, and spices that go best with
it. For example, the Ukrainian soup borscht is a sour soup in
which beets are central. They give the soup its distinctive red
color. Borscht is often seasoned with caraway seeds, dill, black

pepper, and celery seeds. French onion soup is another classic. It is a rich, full-flavored soup made with a meat stock and onions and served with melted cheese on top of a crusty piece of bread. It's seasoned with garlic, thyme, and sherry. From East Asia, hot and sour soup is usually meat-based and often contains ingredients such as daylily buds, wood ear fungus, bamboo shoots, and tofu. Its spiciness comes from chili paste and the sourness from vinegar. Thai cooks make a delicious creamy carrot soup spiced with garlic, chili sauce, coconut, sriracha sauce, and fresh basil.

Other delicious and classic vegetable soups include Italian minestrone soup, Spanish gazpacho, Vietnamese pho, Japanese miso soup, and Cuban black bean soup.

It's fun to be creative and put together your own invention of a mixed vegetable soup. It can be made from vegetables and spices you have on hand, or it can reflect the style and spices of different cuisines. Here are five different variations you can experiment with.

Italian-Style Vegetable Soup

Tomatoes of course are central to Italian cuisine. These pair with a vegetable or light chicken stock. Complementary vegetables that you could use include green beans, roasted artichokes, peppers, sweet peas, zucchini, and summer squash. For soup flavorings, try garlic, rosemary, oregano, parsley, basil, or salty parmesan cheese.

Mexican-Style Vegetable Soup

Tomatoes are also celebrated in this cuisine. A delicious Mexican soup could start with a vegetable or light chicken broth, and then vegetables like corn, red and green peppers, onions, tomatoes, carrots, zucchini, black beans, or pinto beans can be added. You could spice this soup with different types and heat levels of peppers, such as chile, ancho, chipotle, paprika, or jalapeño peppers. Herbs could include cumin, coriander, thyme, or fresh cilantro. Add a splash of lime for brightness.

Spicy Vietnamese Vegetable Soup

Vietnamese cuisine celebrates the traditional soup pho, made of a spiced bone broth and noodles. For a vegetarian version, use a light vegetable stock (mushroom based) and dilute with water if needed so the warm spices of cinnamon, star anise, cloves, garlic, ginger, and lemongrass come through. Char some ginger and onion before you add them for a traditional flavor. Add tamari soy for seasoning, and use rice noodles. Add fried tofu if you want. Add vegetables such as butternut squash, green beans, onions, or bean sprouts, as well as enoki or shitake mushrooms. After cooking, garnish the soup with lime slices, jalapeño slices, mint, green onions, or Thai basil.

Eastern European Vegetable Soup

The countries of Eastern Europe—Russia, Poland, the Czech Republic, Hungary, and others—share a flavor and style for their vegetable soup: warm, rich comfort food that simmers for hours on the stove. These soups can pass as a main course. Start with this soup with a rich beef or ham stock. Add the traditional vegetables: potatoes, turnips, beets, carrots, or other root vegetables. Also add cabbage, split peas, onions, or pickles. For seasoning, include a bouquet garni of thyme, parsley, marjoram, leek, celery, and bay leaf. Add garlic, red pepper flakes, paprika, dill, allspice, or other hearty flavors.

North African Vegetable Soup

North African cuisines share a similar flavor profile to that of Spain. Start with a light chicken stock. For vegetables, add zucchini, chickpeas, onion, celery, potatoes, tomatoes, and carrots. The uniqueness of a North African soup comes from an intense flavor combination from multiple herbs and spices, including turmeric, coriander, cinnamon, cayenne, parsley, ginger, saffron, or mint. Add a splash of lemon or lime juice for fresh flavor.

Health Benefits

Vegetable soup is a great way to include vegetables into your diet. Most vegetable soups contain a range of vitamins and minerals along with a balance of carbohydrates, fat, and protein. Vegetable soup can also be a good source of dietary fiber.

Vegetables in general are good sources of many important nutrients, including potassium, dietary fiber, folate (folic acid), vitamin A, and vitamin C. Many also provide vitamin E, thiamin, niacin, vitamin B_6, copper, and manganese. The healthiest vegetables are spinach and other leafy greens; carrots; garlic; cole crops like cabbages, broccoli, and kale; green peas; ginger; asparagus; and sweet potatoes. These are vegetables with rich colors and tastes and many uses in vegetable soups.

Some loss of nutrients always occurs with cooking. Some tips to retain maximum vitamin content in soups include using fresh vegetables as soon as possible, not thawing any frozen vegetables before adding them to a soup, keeping cooking times as short as possible, and adding vegetables to the broth after it is already boiling. Stirring soups also tends to reduce nutrients. Tightly cover the soup pot when it's cooking and while leftovers are being stored.

The total calories in vegetable soups is different for every recipe, but most contain about fifty to a hundred calories per one-cup serving. Protein can be found in some vegetables, especially legumes like black beans, lentils, and soybeans (tofu), but it will also come from beef or chicken broth. Most vegetable soups contain low amounts of saturated fat and cholesterol.

You do need to watch out for the sodium in vegetable soups. Prepared vegetable soups and recipes can be high in sodium. Look for low-sodium recipes or just leave out the salt if this is an issue for you.

Vegetable soup using a poultry or meat broth is a stepping-stone toward reduced meat consumption. Tom Levitt writes that if enough people adopt a diet in which most of the food they consume is vegan (lots of vegetables and small amounts of animal products), we can contribute to reducing emissions that cause climate change. Something as simple as eating more vegetable soup can be a part of this process.

My Soup Garden for Next Year

Okay, now I'm definitely hungry for a bowl of soup! Next time I plant a soup garden, I think I'll spice it up with a few recipes from around the world. I'd like to grow distinctive aromatic spices, such as lemongrass, ginger, turmeric, paprika, dill, papolo, pipicha, and cilantro. Also some less common vegetables, such as okra, bean sprouts, beets, and sweet potatoes. I think a good combination of soup recipes might be Russian borscht, Vietnamese pho, and maybe an Indonesian soup with ginger, turmeric, and lemongrass. I'll look for some delicious new recipes this winter.

Resources

Levitt, Tom. "Why Going Vegetarian Isn't Necessarily the Best Diet for the Planet." HuffPost. September 16, 2019. https://www.huffpost.com/entry/vegan-vegetarian-climate-change-diets_n_5d7fa569e4b03b5fc8873dc7.

Taylor, Kathryne. "Redeeming Green Soup with Lemon and Cayenne." *Cookie and Kate* (blog). June 28, 2019. https://cookieand kate.com/redeeming-green-soup-with-lemon-and-cayenne.

"Why Is It Important to Eat Vegetables?" United States Department of Agriculture. Accesssed January 30, 2020. https://www.choose myplate.gov/vegetables-nutrients-health.

La Dolce Vita: Italian Citrus Fruits

➤ Natalie Zaman ➤

My nonna never learned to speak English. She was from a little town called Amantea in the region of Calabria on the west coast of southern Italy. She came to America in the 1920s through Ellis Island and spent the next several decades living in the Lower East Side of Manhattan. New York City, even then, couldn't be more different than where she was from. From what I've been told, she adapted well to city life; maybe it was because there were so many other Italians around. It was life in the suburbs that disturbed her—specifically, the front and back yards. She *hated* lawns.

"All this grass," she told my mother. "*Che spreco!*—what a waste!" Why wasn't all that space used to grow

vegetables? There was plenty of room in the suburban sprawl for orchards, grape vines . . . even flowers. Anything but turf. That was only good for goats, and you didn't see any of them, not in our neighborhood.

I have yet to see Amantea. The furthest south in Italy I've ever been is Positano—that pastel-building-encrusted cliffside town that's on a million Pinterest boards. It boasts a patch of flat seaside and lots of tourists on its narrow streets. There isn't a lot of room, but somehow the plants, the flowers, and, of course, the fruit were everywhere. Green spilled over every ledge. As our bus careened around corners with a hundred-foot drop on one side and a tightly packed village on the other, we passed pairs and trios and groves of olive trees, all festooned with nets underneath their branches to catch the ripening fruit. And then there were the lemon trees (more on these later). They lined every lane—just like elms on an American Main Street. Every one was heavy with fruit (I would see lemons as big as footballs!). I was in Italy at the height of the summer, and the ubiquitous citrus that was everywhere captured my senses and imagination. The fat blonde orange I bought at a market in Rome, the incense-infused tartness of bergamot in the perfume I picked up in Florence, and all those lemons in Positano—when I stepped out of the bus, I could practically taste them.

Italians love fruit. Seriously. According to Katia Amore in an article for *ITALY Magazine*, in 2010 Italians ate more fruit than their European counterparts (*mela e arance*—apples and oranges—are their favorites), and they're efficient about it too. Nonna didn't care for waste, and when it comes to any kind of produce, every part is used: seeds are planted; flesh is eaten, pulped, and juiced; and skins and rinds hold the precious oils that often give fruit its heady flavor and scent. Italian fruits are pressed and processed to yield all sorts of marvelous things, as I discovered and as you shall see . . .

Arance!

I grew up on Florida oranges—were there ever any others? That's what was on offer in the produce department and in the cartons of juice at the grocery store. When my aunt and uncle started going to Florida for the winter, they'd send boxes of oranges straight from the grove. (It's where I got used to "imperfect" fruit. Note that good-looking does not always equal delicious when it comes to any kind of produce!) Sicily is Italy's top producer of oranges, and these oranges generally fall into two categories: blonde and blood. Blonde oranges are your typical sunny-skinned orange-yellow-fleshed fruit—and very like what I bought at the Roman market stall. Blood oranges are, by their nature and name, more intriguing.

Sicilian blood oranges, *arance rosse di Sicilia*, hit the markets in December and are at the height of production through early summer. They come in three varieties, each darker in flesh than the next: *tarocco, moro,* and, the bloodiest of all, *sanguinello*. Tarocco is the lightest and sweetest of the three. Its pink flesh has no seeds and has more vitamin C in it than any other orange in the world, probably because of the super rich volcanic soil created by Mt. Etna. Moro is a bit darker, and sanguinello, darker still. These oranges have a berry-tinged flavor that is deeper and stronger than their lighter-fleshed sisters.

Blood Orange Syrup

While the straight-up juice is lovely on its own, blood orange syrup will add a drop of sunshine to any dish or drink that needs a bit of *dolce*-fication.

Mix 2 parts juice to 1 part sugar. Bring the mixture to a boil over a low flame, stirring constantly until it thickens (about 15–20 minutes). The syrup can be used to flavor drinks or drizzle over cakes, yogurt, oatmeal, or any dish to which you want to add a bit of sweetness. For flavor variations, add 2–3 cloves, a small stick of cinnamon, or a vanilla pod while cooking the syrup. The syrup should keep for up to 2 weeks in the refrigerator.

Spicy Orange Potpourri

Oranges—blood or otherwise—aren't just for eating. When I was in Florence, I visited the Officina Profumo-Farmaceutica di Santa Maria Novella, one of the world's oldest perfumeries. They began operations in the thirteenth century and have been producing items for the public for a little over 400 years! The *farmacia* was originally run by monks who created medicines using the natural ingredients that were at hand. Among their remedies is potpourri, a medieval protective against the plague. Save your orange peels to make a spicy potpourri that may not ward off illness but can smell like Christmas.

In this blend, I'm trying to re-create the scent of the molded wax nativity scene I bought in Florence. Save your orange peels and air dry them, which will take a couple of days, or dry them in a low oven (170°F) for a few hours. Simply place the following ingredients into a mason jar, seal it, and shake it:

1 cup dried orange peel

¼ cup cloves

1–2 cinnamon sticks, broken up

¼ cup of star anise

A few drops of orange oil

1–2 drops of cinnamon oil

The longer you leave the scents to infuse, the more intense they will be. Feel free to adjust the amount of spices used to your taste. You can also include unscented wood shavings to bulk it up. The potpourri can be refreshed or altered by adding additional drops of essential oils.

Battaglia delle Arance

Just before Lent, the city of Ivrea goes a bit crazy for oranges—or rather, with oranges. In the *Battaglia delle Arance,* as the story goes, the citizens hurl oranges at each other—nearly 400 tons of fruit leftover from the winter crop. Why? About 800 years ago, Ivrea was ruled by a wicked duke. The townspeople rose up in anger and knocked down his castle by throwing stones at it. The catalyst for the uprising was a miller's daughter with whom the duke tried to claim the right of *prima nocta,* the right of an overlord to spend a night with a newly married woman before her husband. In this case, the miller's daughter turned the first night right to her own advantage by cutting off the duke's head, thus starting a revolution. The festival is a reenactment of the demolition of the castle. Each year, women vie for the role of "Violetta" (the miller's daughter), and orange-hurling teams vie for prizes (and bruises!). Celebrants started by throwing beans, then apples, at each other. It wasn't until the nineteenth century that oranges symbolically took the place of the stones that tore down the duke's castle.

Limoni!

Sicilian designers Dolce and Gabbana have a love of lemons. They put them on dresses, bags, and shoes, and their various lines, especially of late, pay homage to their southern Italian roots where lemons rule (almost!) all. Besides the lemon trees that lined the streets, everything in Positano seemed to have a lemon on it or in it. Shops sold lemon pastries. Sandals and jewelry were studded with tiny crystal and glass lemons. Plates, platters, and jugs were painted with lemons (and fish—not surprising, as Positano is a seaside town). It is interesting, however, that a trick to negate the smell of fish on one's hands—if you handle a fish, you inevitably smell of fish—is to halve a lemon and rub it over your fingers and hands.

Where there are that many lemons, inevitably you will find *limoncello*. Limoncello is a distinctly southern Italian drink. There are those who will argue that Sicily makes the best limoncello, but I was rather fond of what I found in Positano. Sorrento lemons, or Femminello St. Teresa lemons, are the fruit of choice for making limoncello because of the high content of oil in their zest.

Limoncello

You can make your own limoncello at home. It only takes about 30 minutes of prep time and at least a month for the flavors and alcohol to infuse. You'll need:

10–12 lemons

3 cups of 100-proof vodka

2 cups sugar

2 cups water

First, take off the top layer of the lemon peel and scrape off any pith (the white part), which will impart a bitter flavor. Place the peels in a jar or bottle, add 1½ cups vodka, and seal it. Steep the peels in the vodka for about 2 weeks. When the peels have paled or lost most of their color, you're ready for the next step.

Make syrup by adding the sugar to the water and bringing the mixture to a boil. Remove it from the heat and let it cool. Strain the peels from the now lemon-infused vodka. Add the other half of the vodka and the cooled syrup. Put your newly minted limoncello into bottles, seal them tightly, and store them in the refrigerator for at least a week before drinking.

Limoncello is traditionally stored in the freezer. Be careful if you do this, as there is a chance that the bottle may burst if it is overfilled, which is why I play it safe and just keep it in the fridge.

Citrons

Another lemon treat you can make that will give you a taste of Italy is candied peel, or citrons. Confession: I've never been a fan of these sweet bits of fruit until I had them in Italy. We'd stopped to have a *taza a café e dolce* (a cup of coffee and something sweet). I ordered my mother's favorite pastry, *sfogliatella*, a flaky shell-shaped pastry filled with ricotta cream that's studded with citrons. I avoided this sweet treat at home because, in my humble opinion, the citrons ruined it. Done right, the outer layer of the pastry will be thin, crunchy, and light, and the cream, also light, should have a subtle citrusy, cinnamon flavor. My experience was the nasty surprise of biting into a gummy, overpowering flavor-bomb—so I avoided these, but I had to at least try it in Italy, for Mom's benefit. The *pasticceria* in Rome nailed it—my guess is because what I had there was made fresh. Also, *cedro* lemons, that giant lemon variety I referred to earlier, were probably used to make them. The difference is in the skin: cut open a cedro lemon and you'll find a thick rind and lots of pith, which makes it perfect for candying.

Candied citrons are easy to make, and you can substitute other fruits for cedro lemons, which may not be readily available. (Try this with oranges and then dip the candied peels in dark chocolate—*delicioso*!). You'll need:

6–10 pieces of fruit

Water

1½ cup sugar (I like to use caster sugar as it's a bit finer than regular sugar.)

Cut the peel off the fruit. When you prepped the lemon peels for limoncello, you avoided the pith—this time leave it on the fruit. No worries about bitterness here, as there is lots of sugar involved! Slice the peels into long, thin strips, and then place them into a pot of boiling water to soften them up (this should take about 10 minutes). Drain them and set them aside. Next, take 1 cup of the sugar, add it to 1 cup of water, and bring it to a boil. Add the peels and stir the pot until the syrup thickens (another 10 minutes). Remove the peels and lay them out on a wire rack to dry for about 1 hour, then coat them with the remaining sugar.

Bergamotto di Calabria!

I thought I knew what bergamot was, but really, I had no clue. I knew bergamot from Earl Grey tea. The scent and flavor is unique and not immediately identifiable (at least to me):

citrusy and a bit incense-y. I actually thought it was an herb, but it isn't: it's a citrus fruit, small, green, and sour. And you don't eat it or juice it. Bergamot's flavor and essence lies in its skin—and about 90 percent of the bergamot consumed in the world comes from Calabria, my nonna's home region.

Bergamot is an evergreen. It's possible that the plant was imported from China and is a cross between an orange and a super sour lime. A tree will provide fruit in about five years, and to give you an idea of how precious the fruit is, a year's crop from a single tree is about 220 pounds of fruit, but it takes about double that to make just four cups of bergamot oil. There are references to the use of bergamot oil in the seventeenth century, but production became refined in the nineteenth century with the invention of the "Calabrian machine."

For about 200 years, bergamot oil was extracted manually by sponge. The fruit was cut in half and the pulp was removed. The remaining skin was rubbed against a natural sea sponge which absorbed the oil—as you can imagine, a long, labor-intensive process and not the most efficient way to extract the oil. The Calabrian machine streamlined the process and also yielded a finer product. It worked something like this: The surface of the fruit was rubbed with two cups. A fixed cup with metal points held the skin and forced out the oil from pressure applied by the second, rotating.

Bergamot oil can be used to make perfume as well as pastries; it imparts that unique flavor to dough and fillings that you taste in Earl Grey tea. Try adding a drop or two of bergamot extract or food-grade essential oil into cake mixes or pastry dough to add a subtle flavor. Seriously—only a drop or two. One drop equals a heaping tablespoon of fruit zest!

Bergamot Marmalade

If you can get your hands on about 2 pounds of bergamot fruit, try making some bergamot marmalade (lovely on toast with butter!). It's easy and quick and almost never fails to thicken (citrus fruits gel naturally). You'll need:

About 2 pounds of bergamots

About 1½ pounds of sugar

Slice the bergamots and place them in a saucepan with the sugar and bring to a boil. (For smoother marmalade, chop up the fruit and pulse it in a food processor before adding to the sugar.) Pour the mixture into sterilized jars, lid the jars, and store them in the refrigerator.

Selected Resources

Amore, Katia. "Foodie Guide to Arance! (Oranges)." *ITALY Magazine*, January 15, 2010. https://www.italymagazine.com/featured -story/foodie-guide-arance-oranges.

"Bergamotto di Reggio Calabria." Made in South Italy Today. Accessed September 1, 2019. http://www.madeinsouthitalytoday .com/bergamotto-di-reggio-calabria.php.

Carey, Sarah. "Candied Citrus Peel." Martha Stewart. May 16, 2017. https://www.marthastewart.com/355599/candied-citrus-peel.

Dini. "Vanilla Blood Orange Syrup." *The Flavor Bender* (blog), September 13, 2019. https://www.theflavorbender.com/vanilla-blood -orange-syrup/.

Kiefer, Peter. "In Italian Town, Civics Lesson from Annual Orange Battles." *New York Times,* February 19, 2007. https://www .nytimes.com/2007/02/19/world/europe/19iht-web.0219 italy.4642863.html.

Perry, Charles. "Taste of a Thousand Lemons." *Los Angeles Times*, September 8, 2004. https://www.latimes.com/style/la-fo-limon cello8sep08-story.html.

Edible Wild Herbs and Grasses

≥ Suzanne Ress ≤

One early spring morning a few years ago, after running a trail race under a soft rain, I was walking back to my parked car when I passed a man at the edge of the green parking area. He was picking little plant leaves and gathering them in a bag. Curious, I asked him, "What are you picking?"

"*Strigoli*," he said.

I moved closer to him and inspected the leaves of the plant he was collecting.

"Do you eat them?"

"Yes. They're delicious steamed, with olive oil and salt."

I looked again, carefully and with intention, at the plant he called strigoli.

"Now is the time to get them," he continued. "They only last a little while."

Having etched the visual identity of this wild plant into my brain, I said good day to the man and went on to my car and then home.

Later that day, after a shower and lunch and once the rain had let up, I went out into the terraced fields below my front yard with a basket to look for strigoli. Happily, I found several large colonies of this plant growing among the new green grasses and occasional bramble sprouts at the start of the first terrace. I picked enough, pinching the leaf clusters off close to the ground, for what I estimated were two servings' worth, leaving plenty behind in each colony. Later I looked up the word *strigoli* on the internet.

The Latin name for strigoli (which is an Italian familiar name) is *Silene vulgaris*. Known as bladder campion or maiden's tears in English, it is a common flowering wild plant in Europe and North America, where it comes up in fields and grassy places in full sun in the early spring. It is tender and tasty, cooked or raw, at the start of the season, but later it will bloom with bell-shaped pink or white flowers and is better left alone.

Tips for Foraging

I've always been attracted to the idea of foraging for, or simply coming across, wild edibles and incorporating them into my diet. Like most people, I love finding a patch of wild blackberries, blueberries, or cloudberries along the trails in the woods, and in the autumn I do purposefully take hikes to collect wild nuts and mushrooms, but until that moment when I encountered the strigoli man, I hadn't given much thought to identifying and gathering what turns out to be a huge abundance of wild greens and grasses that are literally surrounding us.

That said, the number-one rule to keep in mind when foraging for wild food plants is to know you are positively identifying what you are collecting. You must have no doubt! Many plants that look similar to edible plants can be toxic and make you sick, so I cannot emphasize enough how important it is to be absolutely sure that what you gather with the intention of eating is, in fact, edible! The best way to be certain is to check and double check on the internet, carefully observing numerous images and very carefully reading the plant's description, until a specific plant becomes so familiar to you that your eyes pick it out from a field full of hundreds of different plants.

And there really are hundreds of different delicious edible plants out there. When I take one of my haltered horses into a semi-wild grassy field, he will sample many different plants. And it often happens, as I watch the horse's enthusiasm, that my own appetite is ignited. *I wonder what that one tastes like,* I think. *It sure looks green and tender. And if my horse eats it, perhaps I can too.* I sometimes do end up tasting many of the wild grasses while standing around such a place with one of my horses. Plantain, dandelion greens, curly dock, valerian, wild rocket—it's a gigantic outdoor salad bar.

Wild greens and grasses usually have much stronger, more distinctive flavors than the domesticated salad greens you might buy in a supermarket. This is because they are much higher in natural plant alkaloids, which is also what makes the edible ones so good for you, according to forager and educator Leda Meredith.

There are many excellent informative websites for identifying wild plants. I recommend these:

- basisgear.com
- eattheplanet.org
- wildedible.com
- Wild Edibles Lite (App)
- wildernesscollege.com
- wildernessawareness.org

Wild Greens

As a young child, I lived with my family in a house with a forest abutting the backyard. We kids were not allowed to go into the woods alone, and I (mostly) did not, although I thought that the border between the woods and the yard didn't count as woods, and sometimes the border area seemed quite wide. At the edge of the yard and into the border there were long grasses and plants that never got mowed down.

Wood Sorrel

One of these that I discovered to be very tasty was wild wood sorrel. I don't remember how I discovered its slightly sour, lemony taste, but I frequently munched on the leaves. Their taste is unlike anything else. Not exactly sour, not tart, not acidic, not vinegary—and yet, all those flavors and more. Only much later did I learn that wild sorrel has oxalic acid, the same thing that's found in spinach and in chocolate.

Plaintain

Plantain (*Plantago*) is one of the easiest wild salad greens to find. It grows almost everywhere, even in cracks in the road, and in most untreated lawns, it is plentiful. Plantain leaves, either *Plantago lanceolata* or *Plantago major*, can be gathered up as the entire rosette form they grow in. Pull up a little of the root to keep the leaves together, and cut it off. After thorough washing in cold water, the young leaves are delicious chopped up into mixed green salads. Older leaves should be steamed or eaten plain, or they can be added to eggs, soups, rice, stews, or pasta. I find that plantain has a somewhat salty taste, and this is probably due to its high flavonoid and mineral content.

Make sure never to eat anything from lawns or other areas that have been treated with pesticides, and this includes maintained roadsides. Even unmaintained roadsides are not advisable foraging places, as the plants there are likely to be dirty and may have absorbed motor vehicle fumes or been exposed to other chemical or biological filth.

Alliums

At the height of springtime there is a place I sometimes walk or ride my horse to, where the woods floor is moist and the sunlight shines through in mottled patches. Just weeks earlier, the little plants growing there were exposed to full sun. Even from a distance, the scent of garlic and onions is heavy in the air.

Ramps (*Allium tricoccum*) are a lily-of-the-valley look-alike that can be cut off just at the top of the bulb (don't take out the whole bulb!) so the leaf cluster stays together. Leaving the remainder of the bulb in the ground will ensure that the ramps return again next spring. They are delicious cooked in risotto, omelets, or just by themselves, dressed with olive oil and salt.

Other wild members of the *Allium* genus are wild garlic (*Allium sativum*) and wild chives (*Allium schoenoprasum*). For a similar flavor, I also recommend garlic mustard (*Alliaria petiolata*). In general, any plant that smells oniony is edible, but always check your guide first.

Purslane

Purslane (*Portulaca oleracea*) contains omega-3 oils, potassium, calcium, and iron and is the same succulent "fat-leaved" plant that garden centers sell as a beautiful flowering ground cover. Wild purslane, known as pigweed or duck weed, is mild and pleasant tasting and is best eaten raw in salads anytime of year the greens look fresh.

Chickweed

Similar in appearance to purslane is chickweed (*Stellaria media*), another low-growing, ground-covering "weed" often found lurking around vegetable gardens. Chickweed's leaves are not thick and succulent like purslane, but when they are young and tender, the leaves, stems, and flowers are quite tasty cut up in salads.

Burdock

Burdock (*Arctium*), the rather ugly, big, common weed whose leaves resemble rhubarb leaves, has edible roots and flower stalks. Its leaf stems are also edible but should be peeled before eating. Even its leaves can be eaten, but they are bitter tasting.

Curly Dock

Another dock, curly dock (*Rumex crispus*) is commonly found in wastelands and fields. Its tender spring leaves can be steamed gently and eaten, while older leaves will have to be cooked longer, with several changes of water to remove bitterness.

Springtime Foraging

Many wild greens tend toward bitterness as the season wears on, and because of this, I think spring is the prime time for foraging wild greens and grasses, barring necessity due to possible starvation.

Chicory

Chicory (*Cichorium intybus*), well known for its root in dried form as a caffeine-free coffee substitute, also produces edible leaves. To be edible (meaning not too bitter), they must be picked very early in the spring, shortly after the basal leaves on their rosette form appear above ground. These can be tossed together with young dandelion (*Taraxacum officinale*) leaves to make an unbeatable "spring tonic" salad, chock full of minerals, vitamins, and plant flavonoids.

Thistle

Thistle (*Cirsium vulgare*), also known as Scottish thistle or bull thistle, despite its very spiny appearance, can be eaten when young. Leaves and stems of this plant should be peeled (wear gloves), cut up, and served raw or should be boiled as a vegetable. Its roots can be boiled and then fried like potatoes, although their flavor is less bland and similar to artichokes.

Valeriana

Valeriana (*Valerianella locusta*), commonly known as corn salad or mâche, is a native wild European green that escaped cultivation to become a wild plant in parts of North America. Its young, tender leaves have a nutty flavor and are high in nutrient content, including vitamin C, beta-carotene, B_6, iron, and po-tassium. Its leaves grow in rosettes, which should be twisted off at the base and used whole in salads.

Salad Burnet
Salad burnet (*Sanguisorba minor*), also called pimpinella, has tiny leaves with a refreshing cucumber-like flavor. The leaves are high in vitamin C and are supposed to be good for the di-gestion. These too are best eaten early in the season.

Shepherd's Purse
Shepherd's purse (*Capsella bursa-pastoris*), ubiquitous in vacant yards and empty lots, waste places, and unfertilized fields, pro-duces leaf rosettes with a peppery flavor that blend well, when young and raw, with other, milder spring greens in salads.

Amaranth
Amaranth (*Amaranthus*) has large, broad, and rather ugly leaves similar in size and shape to burdock. These can be eaten young and cooked. Once the plant has flowered and dried naturally, the seeds can be gathered by shaking the plant over a clean piece of fabric. These quinoa-like seeds can be cooked into a porridge or sprinkled over baked goods before they're baked for a crunchy, nutritious topping.

Japanese Knotweed
In most parts of Europe and North America, the extremely in-vasive non-native plant Japanese knotweed (*Fallopia japonica*) is especially satisfying to make use of just because it seems to be everywhere, ineradicable, and otherwise useless. Only the young shoots (up to a foot high) are worth eating. These can be gathered in the spring, their tips steamed or sautéed and

enjoyed with butter and lemon, like asparagus tips. It's best to pull up the entire plant and take it with you. Later, cut off the piece you want to eat and burn the rest. Leaving clippings behind will only aid in its spread.

Asparagus

Wild asparagus (*Asparagus officinalis*) grows in fields, but also in sunny spots in the woods—any not too humid place that offers full to partial sun.

During a horse ride through the woods one day early last spring, a friend accompanying me pointed out a patch of wild asparagus I had not previously noticed, though I'd passed that place many times. Its thin purplish stalks are not at all like the cut and bundled cultivated asparagus spears one finds at the supermarket. Wild asparagus's thin stalks can be snapped off and eaten raw or lightly steamed or sautéed, much like cultivated asparagus. Because this is a perennial plant whose roots remain intact from year to year, once you've located a patch of wild asparagus, it's a good idea to remember where it is for the following year.

Dame's Rocket

Dame's rocket (*Hesperis matronalis*), with its pretty pinkish-purple edible flowers, is the wild cousin of supermarket arugula. Its young, tender leaves are delicious in salads.

Fireweed

Fireweed (*Chamerion angustifolium*) is another tasty salad addition. Use its flowers and young, tender leaves raw. Later, when the leaves get bitter, they can be boiled in several changes of water, and the stalk can be peeled and eaten raw.

Red Clover

The sweet-tasting flowers as well as the young leaves of both the ubiquitous red clover (*Trifolium pratense*) and white clover (*Trifolium repens*) can be eaten raw. This is one wild grass plant that offers edible blossoms all summer long. When the clover leaves get older, it can still be eaten boiled or added to anything cooked, such as omelets, soups, risottos, pasta dishes, and stews.

Cornflower

Another very common wild grass is cornflower (*Centaurea cyanus*). It blooms in the early summer with lovely blue frills of flowers that have a slightly sweet, clove-like flavor. The petals can be torn off the flowers and tossed raw into almost anything, and the whole flowers can be used as edible garnishes.

Late Spring Foraging

As mentioned earlier, the majority of wild greens and grasses are at their best from early to mid-spring, but thereafter they tend to become bitter and tough. There are, however, a few common wild grassy plants that are exceptions, offering something yummy to eat later in the season.

Cattail

One of these is the cattail (*Typha latifolia*), whose young green catkin bloom spikes can be picked before their pollen is ripe. Remove the outer skin, boil until tender, and eat like corn on the cob, with butter and salt.

Mallow

Wild mallow (*Althaea officinalis*), usually found at the edges of marshy places, blooms in the late summer. Before the pretty pink flowers blossom, some of the buds can be harvested and pickled, much like pickled okra, which they resemble.

Keep Your Eyes Open

Once summer comes in and most wild greens have passed their prime, a true all-season forager will concentrate her efforts on wild berry and fruit picking, as these will be plentiful now, along with, of course, whatever you have growing in your vegetable patch.

These are just a few of the hundreds of common wild greens and grasses you can easily find and eat. Next time you are walking through a field or other sunny wild place, look carefully at how diverse the plant life is all around you. You can be certain that, with the right knowledge, you could make a fine meal of these plants.

Happy foraging!

Resources

Department of the Army. *The Official U.S. Army Illustrated Guide to Edible Wild Plants.* Guildford, CT: The Lyons Press, 2003.

Elias, Thomas S., and Peter A. Dykeman. *Field Guide to Edible Wild Plants.* New York: Outdoor Life Books, 1982.

Lust, John. *The Herb Book.* New York: Benedict Lust Publications, 1974.

Meredith, Leda. *The Skillful Forager.* Boulder, CO: Roost Books, 2019.

Seasonings Greetings: Herb and Spice Blends for Meal Planning on a Budget

≽ Mireille Blacke ≼

As a registered dietitian, I'm frequently asked how to "eat better on a budget," because most of us realize that nutrition is important to overall health and well-being, and we also want to make the most of our food dollars. This requires attention to meal planning before shopping, grocery purchasing, and meal preparation.

Plan

Before you hit the store, plan meals for the week and create a shopping list. Make the decision that you will not waver from the list.

Plan to shop for staples, but incorporate versatility. Your list should include inexpensive items with nutritional value, like sweet potatoes, dry

lentils, eggs, squash, and beans. For versatile proteins, chicken and tofu are good choices. Canned beans (like chickpeas) are a great substitute for pricier animal-based proteins. "Going meatless" at least once a week can positively impact your health and food budget.

When creating your list, keep in mind that certain foods are low-cost year-round: beans (black, cannellini, and chickpeas), carrots, greens, potatoes, apples, and bananas. Outside of these foods, follow the general food budget rule that fruits and vegetables in season cost less.

It may be tempting to add frozen dinners, instant foods, or individualized items to your list, but remember that homemade stews and stir-fries stretch into more portions than convenience items. Taking the time to prepare your own food will save you money.

Maybe you aren't into couponing, but most supermarket chains offer customer loyalty cards. Discounts are automatically applied to shoppers who present this card and purchase store brand products. Keep that card with your shopping list. Also, bring reusable shopping bags with you; most stores now charge shoppers for paper or plastic bags.

Purchase

Regardless of your preferred grocery store, don't shop when you're hungry, excessively full, or feeling rushed, crowded, or stressed. Grocery shopping at these times increases your chances of making impaired buying decisions, impulsive spending (resulting in a greater or lesser amount of food), and purchasing foods of inadequate nutritional value.

You made a list for a reason, so avoid aisles that don't contain items on that list.

Compare unit prices for the best deals. Store brands are usually cheaper.

Use the self-checkout. Your chances of impulse buying drop significantly if you do.

Prepare

Select one day a week when you have time (preferably a day off) to precook meals for the household in advance of the upcoming week. By doubling or tripling the recipes you make on this day, you can freeze meals in individual containers for use throughout the week. Having meals on hand saves money by preventing impulsive decision-making when hungry, including money spent on takeout. Turn leftovers into subsequent meals, minimize food waste, and stretch those food dollars even further.

This sounds simple enough, and it works. But after a while of diligent planning, purchasing, and preparation, even savvy shoppers hit a wall. This wall is called boredom.

Seasoning for Savings: Herbs and Spices

If variety is the spice of life, it's also critical in transforming familiar or boring dishes (hello, baked chicken and steamed vegetables) into appetizing leftovers that can extend your food budget. Let's face it: if you're throwing food away, you're throwing money away too.

Many of my clients have hit that wall of boredom, but creatively adding a few herbs and spices greatly benefited their wallets. Simply, herbs and spices allow you to add new life to leftovers, experiment with foods in new ways to create new dishes, and even experience foods from other cultures. All these activities can stretch your food budget dollars.

If you're thinking, *Adding extra herbs and spices is just going to cost me extra time and money!* then keep reading.

Herbs and spices for meal planning on a budget must be versatile, relatively affordable, easy to find, and suitable for "overlapping" culinary purposes. Health and nutrition benefits increase the herb or spice's overall versatility. Therefore, herbs and spices that tend to be expensive (saffron, cardamom, clove), polarizing (i.e., "love it or hate it," such as cilantro), or limited in mainstream availability or culinary usefulness (bay leaves, caraway seeds) do not meet our criteria. Here are some that do:

Basil

Basil is one of the best-known culinary herbs, with sweet basil the most common variety. Basil is rich in potent antioxidants that fight cell-damaging free radicals inside the body. Basil's anti-inflammatory properties help relieve arthritis.

Best With: Tomatoes, cheese (goat, mozzarella), poultry, eggs, vegetables, pesto sauce, sandwiches, soups, and salads (insalata caprese).

Tip: For an easy pesto sauce, blend 2 cups fresh basil leaves, 2 tablespoons pine nuts, ¼ cup parmesan, and ¼ cup olive oil.

Garlic

Garlic is arguably more of a vegetable than an herb, but its culinary uses are extensive. The compound allicin in garlic is associated with enhanced immune function, lowered blood pressure, improved circulation, lower cancer rates, decreased fat storage, improved acne, and memory improvement. Allicin also fights bacteria responsible for stomach ulcers (*Helicobacter pylori*).

Best With: Meats, fish, roasted lamb, salads, salad dressing, pasta sauces, vegetables, bread, and cheese dishes.

Tip: To counter bad breath from the sulfurous compounds in garlic, chew a fresh parsley sprig after a garlicky meal.

Oregano

Oregano is a member of the mint family and a staple in Mediterranean, Cajun, and South American cooking. Oregano is extremely high in antioxidants.

Best With: Tomatoes, lamb, pork, beef, chicken, salads, salad dressings, bean soup, seafood, vegetables, pizza, and sauces.

Tip: Add oregano to vinaigrette for a bolder flavor.

Parsley

Parsley is the herb world's workhorse and fits with just about every food or dish. Parsley contains luteolin, which decreases inflammation in the brain and helps prevent decline in cognitive functions.

Best With: Most foods.

Tip: To make gremolata, chop together equal parts garlic, parsley, and lemon or orange zest. Add this condiment to roasted lamb, grilled steaks, fish, chicken, and vegetables.

Rosemary

Rosemary is one of the most aromatic herbs, known for its lemony pine scent. The age-old belief that rosemary increases cognitive functioning is due to its active ingredient, carnosic acid, which protects against cognitive degeneration, Alzheimer's disease, and stroke.

Best With: Roasted lamb, poultry, pork, grilled meats, vegetables, marinades, breads (focaccia), and tomato sauce.

Tip: Try rosemary on chicken-zucchini skewers or pizza. Keeping in mind rosemary's strong flavor, use a light hand.

Sage

Sage is known for its flavor combination of eucalyptus, cedar, lemon, and mint. Like rosemary, sage is associated with strengthened memory and cognitive skills. The rosmarinic acid in sage protects cells from oxidative damage and helps control inflammation.

Best With: Sausage and bread stuffings, fatty meats, veal, and vegetables.

Tip: Sage can overwhelm a dish; temper it by adding rosemary, parsley, or thyme.

Thyme

Thyme wins the best team player award, playing well with other herbs (particularly parsley, sage, rosemary, and oregano) and a broad range of dishes. Thyme is a cornerstone in Cajun and Creole cooking and a key ingredient in Caribbean jerk seasonings. Thyme is rich in iron, which facilitates oxygen transport in the body.

Best With: Roasted meats, vegetables, marinades, tomato sauce, soups, stews, and scrambled eggs.

Tip: Seasoning with thyme is thought to protect food from bacterial contamination.

Spices

Black Pepper

Black pepper is one of the world's most popular spices, with antioxidant and antibacterial properties. Considered a potent digestive aid and carminative (helping to prevent flatulence), black pepper's sharp flavor signals the brain to produce hydrochloric acid secretion in the stomach, which discourages unhealthy bacterial growth and prevents symptoms of bloating and indigestion.

Best With: All vegetables; all soups; and all poultry, meat, fish, and game. Never discount simplicity; sometimes this is all you need.

Tip: Because increased sodium intake can increase risk for hypertension, cardiovascular disease, and stroke, substitute black pepper for salt in seasoning.

Cayenne

Cayenne is made from a small, spicy red pepper and adds color and heat to foods. Considered a stimulant, antiseptic, and digestive aid, cayenne's active ingredient (capsaicin) is responsible for its heat and is used commonly in topical pain relievers. Hot peppers like cayenne clear congestion, fight cholesterol, and raise metabolism to lower body fat. For those who can handle the heat, hotter peppers indicate higher antioxidant concentration and greater health benefit.

Best With: Sauces, pastas, stir-fries, and Cajun and Indian recipes.

Tip: Avoid touching the eyes after handling cayenne.

Cinnamon

Cinnamon is a versatile aromatic spice with a bittersweet flavor. It is an antioxidant and nutrient powerhouse, shown to protect against inflammation, heart disease, and Alzheimer's disease. Cinnamon consumption is also associated with greater blood sugar control, increased brain functioning and peripheral circulation, and improved digestion and fat metabolism.

Best With: Chili, curries, stews and sauces, ham, sweet potatoes, oatmeal, apples, berries, chicken, rice, pears, chocolate, oranges, nuts, and ground coffee.

Tip: Play with cinnamon's versatility in sweet and savory
dishes.

Note: Minimize cinnamon consumption during pregnancy, as
it may stimulate early contractions.

Cumin

Cumin is a key component in curry powder and packs a nutty
earthiness and peppery punch. Cumin is a cornerstone in
Middle Eastern, Indian, Mexican, and Southwestern cooking.
Cumin has been shown to aid digestion, stabilize blood sugar,
and fight colon, stomach, and liver cancers. Cumin seeds are
high in iron, manganese, calcium, and magnesium, which are
important for energy production and immune function.

Best With: Chili, beans, chicken, couscous, curry, eggs, eggplant, fish, lamb, lentils, peas, pork, potatoes, rice, sau-
sages, soups, and stews.

Tip: Liven up brown rice with cumin, parsley, almonds, and
dried apricots.

Ginger

Ginger is one of the oldest and most popular spices, known
for its zesty, peppery, and fragrant root. Ginger is considered
an antioxidant, antimicrobial, and effective food preservative,
with brain-protective and anti-inflammatory properties. Ginger consumption has been linked to effective treatment of
certain types of nausea, muscle pain associated with exercise,
colon inflammation, and arthritis, though further research is
warranted.

Best With: Gingerbread, baked goods, beverages (ale, tea, beer, wine), sweet potatoes, apples, figs, meats, and tomato soup.

Tip: Add ginger and orange zest to roasted carrots.

Note: Ginger consumption in large quantities may lead to stomach distress and should be avoided by persons taking anticoagulants or with gallstones.

Paprika

A milder relative of cayenne, paprika is ground from red pepper pods and may be sweet or hot. Paprika helps boost the immune system via its high concentration of vitamins A and C. Paprika is considered an antiseptic and digestive stimulant and is linked to improved blood circulation.

Best With: Meats, seafood, roasted chicken, hearty stews, and vegetables; garnish on traditional deviled eggs.

Tip: Embrace paprika's sweet and spicy varieties. Dust paprika on scrambled eggs or mix it into low-fat mayonnaise for a dip.

Note: Large quantities of paprika may aggravate the stomach.

Turmeric

Turmeric, a component of curry, offers an earthy, peppery flavor while providing anti-inflammatory, antimicrobial, antifungal, and cancer-fighting properties. Turmeric's active ingredient (curcumin) has neuroprotective effects on the brain and may be helpful in stroke prevention. Curcumin is also linked with inhibited tumor growth and improved cardiovascular health. Touted by some as the "yellow miracle spice," turmeric is associated with beneficial effects on arthritis, cholesterol profiles, and lowered risk of prostate and colon cancers.

Best With: Rub turmeric onto chicken or fish, coat roasted
nuts with it, or mix it with yogurt, garlic, and ginger to
make a sauce or dip.

Note: Long-term consumption of turmeric may lead to stomach distress.

Practice moderation. Stomach distress is common with large
quantities of ginger, paprika, and turmeric. Ginger in particular may interact with some medications, such as the blood
thinner warfarin (Coumadin). Ginger should also be avoided
in persons with gallstones, as it stimulates bile production.
Avoid the "ginger jitters" (central nervous system excitation)
by keeping intake to less than 2 grams of ginger per kilogram
(1 kilogram = 2.2 pounds) of body weight.

Meal Planning with Herbs and Spices

Use herbs and spices to celebrate your own heritage or favorite
ethnic foods. As well as expanding your menu, adding flavorful combinations of garlic, ginger, cumin, basil, black pepper,
and oregano can replace salt and saturated fat in your meals.

Keep your dried herbs and spices stored in airtight containers, preferably away from heat, steam, and sunlight. Most
have a shelf life of about one year, but if you open that container and can't smell much, chances are you won't taste too
much either!

Consider "blooming" your spices to intensify their flavor.
To do this, heat oil in a frying pan, add spices to the oil and
mix for 3 to 5 seconds. Then add vegetables, meat, and so on
to that oil. Enjoy the enhanced flavor!

Herbs and spices can enhance cooking tremendously, but
begin with a light hand. Less is more; use just enough of an
herb or spice to heighten natural flavors.

Though many supermarket chains have made it easy and affordable to buy herbs and spices in bulk, you may find better deals at international grocery stores.

Time and effort in the areas of planning, purchasing, and preparation are necessary to save money on grocery items. Adding select herbs and spices is a relatively easy and creative way to extend the value of your chosen foods. Your own list will vary based on food preference, but the bottom line is you only need a few to create a variety of dishes.

Here are some recipes to get you started!

Crunch 'N' Munch Roasted Chickpeas

This recipe is fast, inexpensive, versatile, and extremely simple to make. The chickpeas are also extremely portable for taking to work, school, or the gym. Note that if the chickpeas are not dry enough, cooking time is extended and impacts the outcome: the all-important "crunch!" A number of dry seasonings (sweet and savory) work well in this recipe, so try whatever appeals to you.

1 15-ounce can of chickpeas (garbanzo beans)

Nonstick cooking spray

Dry seasoning of your choice: cumin, garlic powder, black pepper, paprika, cayenne, cinnamon, Italian seasoning (recipe follows), cocoa, salt

Drain and rinse chickpeas. Pat them down with paper towels until they are as dry as possible. Cooking time may increase significantly if chickpeas are not dry.

Spray shallow baking pan with nonstick cooking spray.

Place dry chickpeas in shallow baking pan and cover with seasoning of your choice.

Bake at 350°F for an hour or until chickpeas are crisp. The chickpeas will become crunchier as they cool.

Italian Seasoning

There are many versions of Italian seasoning. After reviewing the recipe, you can make a more informed decision about the ingredients and adjust to your taste.

3 tablespoons dried oregano

3 tablespoons dried basil

2 tablespoons dried thyme

2 tablespoons dried rosemary

2 tablespoons dried marjoram (or 1 tablespoon ground)

1 tablespoon dried parsley

½ tablespoon dried sage

Optional:

2 teaspoons garlic powder

1 teaspoon onion powder

Red pepper flakes

Blend together in a blender or a spice grinder for a finer, more uniform seasoning. Keep in a jar or another airtight container.

Best for Last Chili

Chili is the meal that keeps on giving. It's inexpensive to make, easy and quick to prepare, leaves ample leftovers, and is packed with flavor. Moreover, chili recipes can be adjusted for "heat" preferences; herbs and spices take it to the next level. Meat can be omitted to make the meal vegetarian, and the spices can all be replaced with 4 tablespoons homemade chili seasoning (recipe follows). This recipe yields 6–8 servings.

1 pound ground meat (any kind)

2 teaspoons olive oil

2 15-ounce cans of beans, any kind, drained and rinsed

1 28-ounce can diced tomatoes

1 15-ounce can tomato sauce

3 tablespoons chili powder

2 teaspoons ground cumin

2 teaspoons garlic powder

½ teaspoon paprika

½ teaspoon ground pepper

½ teaspoon salt

½ cup broth (any kind) or water

For the slow cooker:
Place all ingredients into a slow cooker and mix. Cover and cook on high for 3–4 hours or on low for 6–8.

For the stove top:
Place olive oil in a large pot and turn to medium-high heat. Add the ground meat and sauté until fully cooked. Add the rest of the ingredients to the pot and bring to a boil. Reduce heat to low and let simmer for 10–15 minutes.

Homemade Chili Seasoning
For additional savings, make your own seasoning for chili recipes, spice/dry rubs, dips, roasted vegetables or meatballs, or whatever you like. Remember, ingredient versatility in the kitchen will help to lower your food costs!

12 tablespoons chili powder

8 teaspoons garlic powder

8 teaspoons ground cumin

2 teaspoons smoked paprika

2 teaspoons salt

1 teaspoon ground pepper

Place all ingredients for the chili seasoning into a large glass container or mason jar. Cover the jar and shake until all spices are combined. Store chili seasoning in a cool, dry place with the jar covered tightly. Makes 4 servings. For extra heat, add cayenne pepper or red pepper flakes. To add sweetness, add 1 teaspoon of brown sugar.

Chili Seasoning for Multiple Recipes

In a typical chili recipe, use around 4 tablespoons of homemade chili seasoning. Lindsey Richter shares these tips for other uses of the mix:

- When using as a rub for chicken, beef, pork, or shrimp, use 1 tablespoon of seasoning per pound of meat.

- For a roasted vegetable side dish, toss a pan of vegetables with olive oil and add 1–2 tablespoons of seasoning. Bake the vegetables at 400°F for 25–30 minutes.

- Mix seasoning into dips or meatballs, or use it as a spice mix for homemade tortilla chips.

Resources

Gurk, Rachel. "Italian Seasoning Recipe." *Rachel Cooks* (blog). May 6, 2019. https://www.rachelcooks.com/2019/05/06/italian -seasoning-recipe/.

Richter, Lindsey. "Homemade Chili Seasoning." *Fit Foodie Finds* (blog), September 3, 2019. https://fitfoodiefinds.com/homemade-chili -seasoning/.

Sandwich Night

❧ Annie Burdick ❧

Every Wednesday night for about seven years, my family ate sandwiches for dinner. Now, I know what you might be thinking. Sounds boring, right? Why would anyone make a big deal about hundreds of PB&Js or ham sandwiches?

It wasn't quite like that. For starters, there wasn't a single white-bread-and-lunchmeat sandwich among the hundreds that graced our plates all those years. These were gourmet and continuously creative. They often fell under specific subcategories: breakfast sandwiches, burgers, wraps, subs, paninis, and the like. And they were beyond delicious.

My stepmom is a culinary school graduate, former chef and caterer, and current owner of two beloved local

bakeries. This woman is the straight-up queen of delicious food. As a result, we were always a foodie family. Despite my sister being the only other one with a natural cooking talent, my dad and I, as a result of their close-quarters culinary influence, also knew enough in the kitchen to whip up some mean sandwiches of our own.

Standard family discussions always came back to food and sandwiches. We regularly discussed the merits of various aiolis and bread types. We debated the pros and cons of arugula and butter lettuce. We chatted about the benefits of toasting the bread versus toasting the full sandwich. We sassily critiqued each other on the style of cutting and cooking onions, the use of too much or not enough cheese (usually not enough—we're Wisconsinites), chicken seasoning blends and homemade sauces, and why a ripe heirloom tomato or particular herb would have elevated the whole sandwich experience. We spent time on our porch discussing new insane themes we could try for Sandwich Night, picking ingredients out of a hat, or considering ultraspecific types of sandwiches we could all try to best each other at making. We were sandwich fiends.

We wrote down every sandwich we ever made, took turns inventing and cooking the sandwiches, and even each gave ratings out of five stars for every one we ate.

Now that my sister and I are both adults, with education and experience in cooking and writing between the two of us, we're working diligently to select the best recipes and write a full-blown Sandwich Night cookbook.

Gourmet Herbal Sandwiches

One thing I realized while sifting through hundreds of delicious sandwich inventions is that many of our best ones have one thing in common: they use fresh herbs. Our crazy sandwich combinations might not be ones you'd invent as a person who doesn't obsess over sandwiches in your free time, but if you want to quickly and easily elevate any sandwich to a new level, consider using some potent and delicious herbs to bring all the flavors together. You might not think of sandwiches and instinctively head to your garden for some herbs, but after reading these recipes, I bet you'll be more inclined to.

Any sandwich recipe can be easily adjusted for a smaller or larger serving size—just use the amount of bread and ingredients that make sense for your sandwich quantity. You may also like your sandwiches more or less heavily loaded with ingredients, so these amounts are merely an average suggestion. Feel free to make your sandwiches heftier or lighter as needed.

The world's most expensive sandwich is a $214 (yes, really) grilled cheese from Serendipity in NYC. The sandwich uses cheese made from the milk of a rare Italian cow. The bread is made with champagne and gold dust. The whole thing is coated in truffle butter and gold leaf.

Ricotta and Fresh Herb Dipping Sandwich

This is a prime example of two super simple ingredients combined with three fragrant herbs to make a much more delicious and stimulating meal. It's a fresh and straightforward sandwich perfect for pairing with soup or dipping sauces.

This simple recipe includes recommended amounts of each ingredient for one sandwich, so you can increase as desired for any number of servings. It's also merely a guideline; if you're using large bread or prefer more or less of a particular herb, go with your gut! This recipe is just an outline for delicious, herby dipping sandwiches. It makes 1 serving and takes about 15 minutes to create.

2 tablespoons butter

2 slices soft Italian or white sandwich bread

¼ cup ricotta cheese

3–4 teaspoons fresh chives, chopped

3 teaspoons fresh thyme, chopped

2–3 teaspoons fresh dill, chopped

Heat a skillet or grill pan over medium-low heat. Butter one side of each slice of bread. Spread ¼ cup of fresh ricotta cheese (or more, if you want a heartier or creamier sandwich) on the non-buttered side of one slice of bread. Top with the chives, thyme, and dill. Close the sandwich with the other slice of bread, butter side up. Place in the pan and cook on each side for 3–4 minutes, or until you've achieved your desired level of toasting.

This is a super customizable and adjustable sandwich base. Take the simple ingredients of ricotta and tasty sandwich bread and mix and match your additional ingredients. Try adding basil, rosemary, parsley, or oregano in addition to or instead of the above herbs. Or add fontina, goat cheese, or other flavorful cheeses to the mix. Dip your sandwich in the homemade soup recipe that follows, or try marinara sauce or pesto.

Simple Homemade Tomato Herb Soup for Dipping

The ricotta and fresh herb dipping sandwich is excellent served with some homemade or store-bought tomato soup. This recipe is for a warm tomato and herb soup, but we served cold tomato and basil soup for the original creation of this sandwich. The recipe makes about 4 servings and takes 35 minutes to create.

½ onion, cut into chunks

2 tablespoons butter or olive oil

2–3 cloves garlic, diced

1 28-ounce can whole tomatoes

1½ cups vegetable stock

1–2 tablespoons salt

Pepper to taste

1 cup milk or heavy cream

½ cup fresh basil, chopped

2 tablespoons parsley, chopped

1 tablespoon chives, chopped

Parmesan, as desired

Place a medium soup pot over low heat. Add the chopped onions, butter, and garlic and sauté for about 10 minutes, stirring often. Add the can of tomatoes, stock, salt, and pepper and bring to a boil. Then reduce heat to low and simmer for about 10 minutes, stirring occasionally.

Use an immersion blender in the pot to blend all ingredients to a smooth consistency. If you don't have an immersion blender, you can move the mixture to a standing blender, blend, then return it to the pot (be careful—the liquid will be hot). Add milk or cream and all chopped herbs. Stir to combine and allow to simmer for another 7–10 minutes, or until desired taste and consistency is achieved. Mix in parmesan at the end, or serve with parmesan sprinkled on top.

Mind-Blowing Peach and Basil Burgers

There are so many glorious flavors combined together in this one sandwich that your mind might actually be blown. The combination of sweet caramelized peaches; salty pan-fried mozzarella; fresh, flavorful basil; and tangy balsamic is almost too good to be true. Toss that on a pretzel bun and you're really outdoing yourself. These sandwiches require a lot of steps, but I promise they're worth every minute. These can easily be made vegetarian by swapping out the beef patties for veggie burgers of your choice. This recipe makes 4 servings and takes about 40 minutes to create.

For the burger:

1½ pounds ground beef (or premade veggie burgers)

Salt, pepper, and other spices if desired

4 pretzel buns

12–15 leaves of fresh basil

¼ cup balsamic vinegar

For the pan-fried mozzarella:

1 8-oz. ball fresh mozzarella (kept very cold until use)

1 egg

¾ cup panko bread crumbs

¼ cup parmesan

Salt

¼ cup all-purpose flour

2 teaspoons cayenne pepper

⅛ cup olive oil

For the caramelized peaches:

2–3 teaspoons honey

2 teaspoons brown sugar

2 teaspoons olive oil

1 ripe peach, cut into thin slices

Start by forming your meat into burger patties. This amount should make 4 standard burgers, but if you want extra-large burgers, sliders, or double patties, plan your meat quantity accordingly. Season patties as you prefer. Salt and pepper are standard, but you may consider also sprinkling on some garlic salt, paprika, or parsley. Cut and toast buns if you prefer. Clean basil leaves and set aside.

Cut your mozzarella ball into medium-thick slices. Crack the egg into a small bowl, and whisk to break the yolk. In another small bowl, combine the panko bread crumbs, parmesan, and a dash of salt. Stir to combine. Place the flour and cayenne pepper in a third bowl.

Heat a grill pan or skillet to medium and coat the pan in a thin layer of olive oil. When hot, place the patties on the pan and cook for about 5 minutes per side, or to your desired (and safe) level of doneness. Internal temps should be around 130°F for medium-rare burgers and 150°F for medium well. As your burgers finish cooking, drizzle the balsamic vinegar evenly over all burgers. Leave them in the pan (with heat off) as you prepare the other ingredients.

In a small bowl, combine the honey, brown sugar, and olive oil. Add the sliced peaches and toss lightly to coat. Place a small pan over medium-low heat and add the peach mixture. Cook about 2–3 minutes, then stir or flip the peaches, cooking for another 2–3 minutes, or until lightly caramelized and softened.

After this, or at the same time, heat another small pan over medium heat and add ⅛ cup of olive oil (or more for a larger pan; you'll want a thin layer of oil that's enough to create a crispy exterior but not drench the mozzarella). Take each slice of cold mozzarella and bread it by dipping first in the flour mixture, then in the egg, and then in the panko mixture. Place in the hot oil immediately after breading and cook 1–2 minutes on each side, or until the breading gets crispy. Make sure to take the cheese off the pan before it completely melts!

Now assemble the sandwich. Place your balsamic-soaked burgers on buns, followed by basil leaves, pan-fried mozzarella, and peaches. Eat while hot.

Pairing suggestion: This fancy burger goes great with a fresh, summery salad. Try one with roughly chopped spinach, arugula, fresh basil, rosemary, goat cheese crumbles, roasted red peppers, walnuts, and balsamic vinaigrette.

Ultra-Glam (but Secretly Simple) Pancetta and Fennel Grilled Cheese Sandwiches

This is a romantic sandwich recipe if I've ever seen one. Know how to impress a date? Tell them you whipped up some pancetta and fennel grilled cheeses with orange-infused butter, then enjoy their reaction. The bonus is that these shouldn't be too messy, the unromantic drawback of some tasty sandwiches.

While the ingredient list may sound fancy, the execution and creation should be manageable even for a beginner sandwich cook. For those unfamiliar, fennel is an aromatic Mediterranean herb that is delicious and edible from bulb to leafy top. This recipe uses the bulb and leafy parts, but the stalks can be saved and used for many other recipes. This recipe makes 2 servings and takes about 20 minutes to create.

¼ cup butter, softened

2 teaspoons orange juice

1–2 tablespoons orange zest

4 large slices sourdough or thick sandwich bread

3–4 ounces pancetta, cut in thin slices or chopped

½ fennel bulb, plus 2 tablespoons leafy portion, chopped

Salt or other seasonings, if desired

2 sandwich-size slices gouda

2 sandwich-size slices fontina

Start by making the orange-infused butter. Place the softened butter in a small bowl and mix in orange juice and orange zest. If the mixture is not thick enough, add more butter to achieve your desired consistency. Spread the infused butter on one side of each slice of bread and set aside.

Heat a skillet over medium heat. Add the pancetta and a small palmful of chopped fennel leaves and cook for about 4 minutes, stirring to cook evenly. When fully cooked, remove from the pan and set aside on a plate (on a paper towel if you want to soak up some of the oil from the meat).

Cut the fennel stalks from the fennel bulb, then chop half the bulb into thin strips or chunks. Heat the same pan used to cook the pancetta to medium-low, add a drizzle of olive oil, and then add the chopped fennel and a sprinkle of salt or any other seasonings you like. Cook for 4 minutes, stirring until the fennel is slightly softened.

Set a large skillet or grill pan over medium heat. Place 2 slices of bread in the pan, butter side down. Quickly top with slices of gouda and fontina, the sautéed fennel, and a hearty scoop of pancetta on each slice. Top both with the other slices of bread, butter sides up. Cook a few minutes and flip when the bread is golden brown. Cook the other side evenly and remove to a plate. Serve with cocktails, orange slices (don't waste the orange!), and a decadent dessert if you really want to impress someone special.

Mediterranean Chicken and Veggie Open-Face Sandwiches

This Mediterranean-inspired sandwich features a hearty helping of delicious fresh vegetables and chicken, all made more flavorful with a seasoning of garlic and fresh oregano. It's a sandwich that screams summer to me: nice and light, plenty of veggies, but heavy on flavor. It's also super versatile, as you can swap out your preferred veggies or remove the chicken to make it vegetarian. Give it a whirl at your next backyard dinner. This recipe makes 4 servings and takes about 25 minutes to create.

2 handfuls sliced mushrooms of choice

2 tablespoons olive oil

Salt and pepper to taste

4 flatbreads of preferred size

1½ or more cups of parmesan hummus (based on personal preference and flatbread sizes)

1 rotisserie chicken, meat separated from bones and shredded (You may have extra meat left over.)

1 red bell pepper, sliced into thin strips

1 cup crumbled feta cheese

½ cup artichoke hearts, chopped into bite-size pieces

5 cloves garlic, minced

¼ cup fresh oregano, chopped

Heat oven to 350°F. Heat a small pan over medium heat and sauté mushrooms in olive oil with salt and pepper for 5 minutes, stirring occasionally. Reduce heat to low and cook another

2 minutes. Remove from heat once softened. Place flatbreads on a baking sheet. Top each with a hearty scoop of hummus, then spread it evenly across the flatbread. Next add chicken, bell pepper, feta cheese, artichokes, and grilled mushrooms in any order and quantity you prefer. Sprinkle minced garlic and chopped oregano over the top of each. Bake for 6–8 minutes, or until they're toasty and heated. Remove from the oven and serve.

Unexpected Grape and Thyme Sandwiches

I know that basically anyone reading this right now is thinking to themselves that I've officially lost it. Who puts grapes on a sandwich? Well, I'm not sure where this revelation came from, but frankly, it worked out, so who am I to question my own genius? It may sound crazy, but most of the best things do. The combination of warm, juicy grapes with fresh, rich thyme and creamy goat cheese is out of this world. This sandwich is decadent as can be but still only uses a few simple ingredients. This recipe makes 4 servings and takes about 15 minutes to create.

- 1 long baguette, or enough for your desired sandwich sizes
- 2–3 tablespoons fresh thyme
- 2 cups fresh red seedless grapes
- 1 tablespoon olive oil
- Salt and pepper, to taste
- 1 tablespoon water
- 1 4-ounce log soft goat cheese (should be enough for 3–5 sandwiches)

Bake or toast the baguette to your desired warmth and crispiness level. If your bread doesn't have its own baking instructions, toast it at 350°F for 6–8 minutes, or until it is pleasantly warm but not super crunchy.

Roughly chop the thyme. Cut each grape in half—this will release the juices during cooking and help them break down. Heat 1 tablespoon of olive oil in a small pan over medium-low heat. When the pan is hot, add the grapes, along with a hearty sprinkle of salt and pepper, 1 tablespoon of water, and about 2 tablespoons of the fresh thyme (reserve a bit for later). Let the grapes simmer for several minutes, stirring occasionally. After about 5 minutes, the grapes will start to break down and will be swimming in their own juices. This is how you'll know they're ready. Remove them from the heat when they're soft but still hold their shape.

Cut your toasted baguette into sections of your desired size, and slice in half (you know, sandwich style). Spread soft goat cheese on the inside of the bottom piece of bread, then spoon your grapes on top. Use a slotted spoon to scoop the cooked grapes out of the pan, or your sandwich will be totally covered in grape juice. Sprinkle another dash of thyme and salt on top of those grapes, as much as you prefer. Close it up and enjoy while it's nice and toasty.

Alternative option: broil the grapes on a sheet pan for a few minutes and enjoy roasted grapes instead of sautéed.

Sun-Dried Tomato and Breaded Chicken Parm Caprese

One of our highest-ranking sandwiches, this flavor-packed herby delight went down in Sandwich Night history. Though we'll never perfectly re-create the original, which received a perfect five-star rating from all of us, this is a delicious version with tons of flavor and a divine pesto that's simple to make. This recipe makes 2 servings and takes about 40 minutes to create.

For the herb sun-dried tomato pesto:

⅛ cup olive oil (add more as needed)

¼ cup dry sun-dried tomatoes (or less if in olive oil)

½ tablespoon balsamic vinegar

1 teaspoon fresh parsley (or ½ tablespoon dry)

1 teaspoon fresh oregano (or ½ tablespoon dry)

2 teaspoons (or more) fresh basil

1 clove garlic

1 tablespoon parmesan cheese

For the sandwiches:

Small loaf or 2 sandwiches' worth of focaccia bread

1 cup Italian breadcrumbs

¼ cup finely grated parmesan

⅛ cup flour

Salt

Pepper

1 egg

Olive oil (enough to coat your pan)

2 chicken breasts, pounded flat

Several slices of fresh mozzarella (about 4 ounces)

Several leaves of fresh basil

First, prep the pesto. In a food processor, combine all pesto ingredients. Pulse for 30 seconds or until you've created a smooth paste. If the mixture is too dry or thick, add a dash of olive oil and pulse again until you achieve desired consistency.

Slice your focaccia or bread of choice, making 2 sandwich-ready portions. If you prefer them toasted, lightly toast.

Ready three shallow bowls. In one, place the breadcrumbs and parmesan. In another, place the flour and a hearty pinch of salt and pepper. In the third bowl, crack and whisk an egg. Place a skillet or grill pan over medium-low heat and coat the pan with a thin layer of olive oil. Next, dredge and batter each chicken breast by coating first in the flour, then in the egg, and finally in the bread crumb mixture, being careful to coat as thoroughly as possible. Place the coated chicken in the warm pan and cook on each side about 3–5 minutes, or until cooked through. Add more olive oil as cooking if needed.

When chicken is about 1 minute from fully cooked, place cheese slices on each breast and let melt before removing the chicken from the pan.

To assemble the sandwiches, spread a layer of sun-dried tomato pesto on the inside of each slice of bread. Top with the breaded chicken and fresh basil leaves. Eat and enjoy!

———

Now that either your mouth is watering from reading about these sandwiches or you're stuffed from eating one of them, I imagine you're fully on board with the idea of packing your sandwiches with lots of fresh herbs. I've found it to be one of the easiest ways to elevate a simple sandwich in a few seconds. Proven time and time again, sandwiches are one of the most versatile foods you can eat. They never have to be as gourmet as an $18 restaurant burger to be insanely delicious. These recipes, at the very least, are proof of that.

All-Natural Princess Cakes

☞ Linda Raedisch ☜

For years, I'd wanted to make a princess cake. I've always been a fan of Sweden, land of lingonberries, deep forests, and troll-ridden mountains, and I've been there many times in books, poring over histories of eighteenth-century manor houses, gathering wild berries with Astrid Lindgren's *Ronia, the Robber's Daughter,* and rambling through Farmer Pettson's overgrown garden in Sven Nordqvist's hilarious picture books. Making a princess cake, a quintessentially Swedish dessert, would, I hoped, bring me even closer to the land of my dreams.

So what took me so long? For one thing, princess cake is green, and I have an inexplicable aversion to

artificial coloring. For another, princess cake is a fragile construction of sponge, cream, raspberry jam, and marzipan that you are to assemble upside down in a bowl and then turn out into a perfectly smooth dome. There is no room for error, and in the kitchen, I'm all about error. To top it all off, literally, you're supposed to adorn your finished princess cake with a handmade pink fondant rose, a task which requires yet another skill set I do not possess.

Of course, the tradition has always been open to interpretation. The Swede Shop at IKEA sells individual-serving princess cakes. The icing is pink with a drizzle of chocolate, and there are no roses. I do not like these cakes; they are too sweet, too creamy, and entirely too pink for me.

The Cake

Two years ago, I found myself in the position of having to make something impressive looking, easy to serve, and easy to eat for an author event, so I came up with my own recipe for princess cakes. Hardly anyone bought my book, but everybody loved my two-bite (some would argue one-bite) cakes.

In the recipe that follows, I use a traditional sponge recipe, but feel free to substitute your own favorite sponge, jelly roll, or even yellow cake mix. A mix cake will be easier to cut into small rounds, as we are going to do, but it is also slightly more fragile. Either way, it's really the filling that counts.

The Jam

I was nervous about making my own jam, but the process turns out to be surprisingly simple: all you need are berries and sugar. Since raspberries are a soft fruit and contain relatively little pectin, you'll have to cook it for half an hour or more, so I recommend making it a day or two ahead. It won't last as long as store-bought jam, but neither will your princess cakes, and the tartness of my recipe offsets the sweetness of the cake. Raspberry jam is traditional, but since we're already playing fast and loose with tradition, here are some equally Swedish alternatives you might want to consider:

Lingonberries

It used to be I could find lingonberry preserves only at IKEA or our local Scandinavian Christmas market. Recently, I've been seeing them in the grocery store. The lingonberry (*Vaccinium vitis-idaea*), or cowberry, is a wild, tundra-loving member of the heather family, and its branches are used as the base of the candle crown worn by the Christmastime Lucia figure—you can't get much more Swedish than that!

Queen's Blend

Another Swedish phenomenon is "Queen's Blend": raspberries and blueberries eaten together. You can buy Queen's Blend preserves in a jar or mix raspberries and (preferably wild) blueberries together to make your own jam.

Blueberries and Bilberries

The blueberries you get in the grocery store (*Vaccinium corymbosum*) are native to North America. The blueberries in the Swedish Queen's Blend (*Vaccinium myrtillus*) are more properly called "bilberries" and are native to Europe. The famous Bronze Age Egtved Girl, whose 3,000-year-old remains were found in an oak coffin in Denmark, was sent on her final journey with a bucket of wheat beer sweetened with bilberries and honey.

Blueberries, bilberries, and lingonberries are all members of the heath family, while raspberries belong to the rose family and originated in East Asia. Wild raspberries had arrived in Scandinavia by the Viking Age, but it's not certain if Egtved Girl would have known them back in 1370 BCE.

The Marzipan

We need not go all the way back to the Bronze Age for the origins of princess cake. Even the medieval robber's daughter Ronia would not have heard of it; the recipe was pioneered by celebrity baker Jenny Åkerström in the 1930s. At the time, Sweden had three princesses: Margaretha, Märtha, and Astrid. Åkerström baked the first princess cake, or something similar, in honor of Astrid's birthday. Maybe green was Astrid's favorite color. Åkerström used food coloring, but one of the best greens the natural world has to offer is matcha, Japanese green tea powder, and that's what I use to color the outer marzipan shells of my princess cakes. In the tea ceremony, this bright green powder is whisked into a bowl of hot water and drunk as a slightly bitter chaser after the sweets. In my recipe, this bitterness acts as a foil to the sugar in the marzipan.

Don't imagine that you can buy ordinary green tea leaves and grind them into your own matcha in a mortar and pestle. Tea leaves destined for matcha are given special care while still on the bush. Shortly before harvest, they're shrouded in bamboo straw, then they're picked and steamed—not roasted, as Chinese teas are—and milled to a fine powder.

All-Natural Princess Cakes

For the raspberry jam:

> 12½ ounces frozen raspberries
>
> 5 ounces sugar

For the sponge cake:

> ¾ cups white flour
>
> 1 teaspoon baking powder
>
> ½ teaspoon salt
>
> 4 eggs, separated
>
> ¼ cup sugar, plus ½ cup
>
> ½ teaspoon vanilla extract
>
> ½ teaspoon almond extract
>
> Butter to grease pan

For the cream filling:

> ½ pint heavy whipping cream
>
> ¼ cup confectioner's sugar

For the marzipan shell:

> 8 ounces marzipan ("almond candy dough"), found in the baking aisle
>
> 1 teaspoon matcha (equivalent to amount used for one cup of tea)

Tools and utensils:

> Sifter or sieve
>
> 13-by-9-inch baking pan or jelly roll pan (the smaller the pan, the higher the cake)
>
> Electric mixer

Dosing cup, like you get with over-the-counter cold
medicine, or shot glass

Plastic wrap

Egg cup

Small pestle (optional)

Bowls, lots of bowls

Start with the jam. Put frozen berries and ½ cup sugar in a
pot and heat on low until the berries are thawed and sugar
dissolves. Continue cooking, stirring often, on medium heat
for about 35 minutes. You will notice a pink foam forming on
top. Keep stirring it back in. Let the jam bubble along mer-
rily, but keep watch to make sure it doesn't erupt out of the
pot. When it's thick like porridge, remove from heat. When it
stops bubbling, pour it into a bowl or mason jar and let cool.
Keep refrigerated until ready to use.

To make the cake, sift flour, baking powder, and salt into
a large bowl. Set aside.

In a deep bowl, beat egg whites and ¼ cup sugar on low
speed until sugar is dissolved. Increase speed and continue
beating until stiff peaks form. (If you've been beating for 10
minutes and you still can't get stiff peaks, don't worry; it all
gets mixed together anyway.) Cover and set aside. You do not
need to wash the beaters before the next step.

In another bowl, beat egg yolks, extracts, and ½ cup sugar
until mixture is thick and uniform yellow. Fold this mixture
into the flour, then add meringue (those egg whites that you
worked so hard to beat). The batter will be thick. Stir the meringue in as gently but as thoroughly as you can.

Grease the pan and spread the batter in it. The first time I
made this recipe, I realized too late that my jelly roll pan was

a size too large, but since the batter was stiff, I just spread it in a rectangle in the middle of the pan, and it held its shape through baking.

Bake at 375°F for 15 minutes or until golden and firm. (No need to preheat the oven: save energy!)

Wash and dry the beaters.

While the cake is cooling (you can even make it a day ahead), you can make the filling. Whip the cream and confectioner's sugar in yet another bowl until it's thick enough that a blob dropped from a spoon holds it shape. Cover and refrigerate.

Once the cake is cool, cut it into small circles with the dosing cup or shot glass. (Save the scraps!) Spread each round with jam and set them aside while you color the marzipan.

Marzipan dries out quickly, so have a sheet of plastic wrap at the ready before you open the package. In a bowl or on a clean board, knead the dry matcha into the marzipan. Keep kneading until it's a uniform green. Form into a ball and wrap in plastic.

Line an egg cup with a small piece of plastic wrap. If you're lucky enough to have helpers, give a lined egg cup to each. Assemble all your ingredients on the table or counter.

Take a chunk of green marzipan and mold it into a ball the size of a very large marble. Place it in the egg cup and use your fingers or a small pestle to press it into a thin shell. Fill the shell with a spoonful of whipped cream, then gently press a cake round, jam side in, on top. Lift the plastic out of the egg cup and unmold your first little princess cake upside down onto a plate. Return the plastic wrap to the egg cup for the next cake.

You'll probably run out of marzipan before you run out of jam or whipped cream. That's okay. The morning after your fancy tea or garden party, when the princess cakes are all gone, you can eat the leftover jam and cream with the cake scraps for breakfast.

———————

One of these days, I'll try making this recipe as a traditional single-dome princess cake. It might come out all right. Then again, it might be like the time Farmer Pettson set out to make a "pancake cake" for his cat's birthday. Either way, I'm not making that fondant rose. I'll go out to the garden and pick a real one instead.

Health
and
Beauty

Using Aromatic Herbs as Medicine

✎ Holly Bellebuono ✎

We all love deeply inhaling mints: catnip, spearmint, peppermint. They smell incredible, and it's hard to resist inhaling a second time or even a third. The minty fragrance is enlivening and uplifting, and drinking a hot cup of mint tea on a cold day is invigorating, as is drinking a cold glass of iced mint tea on a hot day.

The value of this aroma doesn't stop there. In fact, fragrant herbal medicines are used in formulas to help support our bodies during times of illness or stress.

An herb's very fragrance places it in the category **aromatic**—a group of plants that I've found can be relied upon to medicinally support three primary body systems: the nervous system, the respiratory system, and the digestive system.

For instance, the herb yarrow is a lovely flower that grows wild by the sides of the road and in open fields; it is also cultivated and can be found with white, yellow, or pink flowers. It makes a refreshing—though slightly bitter—tea, and its fragrant leaves are pleasant to smell. But because of its aroma, we know we can rely on yarrow to provide a very specific range of functions for nervous debility, bronchial congestion, and indigestion.

If you have an aromatic herb, chances are high that it is beneficial for all three of these body systems. Other examples of aromatic herbs include fennel, sage, bee balm, lemon balm, catnip, spearmint, motherwort, thyme, oregano, hyssop, and angelica. While each of these is unique and has its own set of actions, they are all aromatic and can generally be counted on to support these three body systems.

Aromatics for the Nervous System

Often the very act of smelling the wonderful aroma of a scented herb is enough to lift the spirits. But herbal remedies go deeper than that, directly addressing anxiety and mild-to-moderate depression. The herbs listed in the following table are often effective in cases of grief and loss, especially combined with rose petal; they also support those with poor memory and recall and with failing cognitive ability, acting as vasodilators and creating a pathway for oxygen to move freely, allowing cognition to peak.

Aromatics are a top choice for children, as most of these herbs are quite safe and have a long-standing traditional history

Aromatic Herbs	
Common Name	Botanical Name
Angelica	*Angelica archangelica*
	A. sinensis
Bee balm	*Monarda* spp.
Cardamom	*Elettaria cardamomum*
Catnip	*Nepeta cataria*
Cinnamon	*Cinnamomum verum*
Fennel	*Foeniculum vulgare*
Ginger	*Zingiber officinale*
Holy basil (tulsi)	*Ocimum sanctum*
Horehound	*Marrubium vulgare*
Hyssop	*Hyssopus officinalis*
Lavender	*Lavandula* spp.
Lemon balm	*Melissa officinalis*
Lemongrass	*Cymbopogon citratus*
Motherwort	*Leonurus cardiaca*
Oregano	*Origanum vulgare*
Peppermint	*Mentha ×piperita*
Sage	*Salvia officinalis*
Spearmint	*Mentha spicata*
Thyme	*Thymus vulgaris*
Yarrow	*Achillea millefolium*

of use. I like to use aromatic catnip for young children who have difficulty sleeping; because it is slightly sedative, catnip combines sedation with nervous system support to help ease a frightened child to sleep, which is very useful for children who are scared of the dark or nervous about being left alone. Let the child pick his or her own catnip leaves and participate in making a warm tea or an infused milk; being involved in the process can be empowering and gives the child a sense of self-agency.

Bedtime Hot Milk

To support an anxious child, catnip combines well with rose, ashwagandha, and a hint of either vanilla or cocoa. Let the child help make the recipe as much as possible.

    1 cup milk (dairy or plant-based)
    1 cup fresh (or ¼ cup dried) catnip leaves, chopped or
        crumbled
    1 teaspoon ashwagandha powder (optional)
    1 teaspoon cocoa powder (optional)
    ¼ teaspoon vanilla extract
    Tiny bit of honey, to taste (optional)

In a saucepan on the stove, gently warm the milk, being careful not to scald it or let a skin form. While warming, place the catnip leaves in the pot; this will infuse the leaves into the milk. Warm for 15 minutes, stirring frequently. Strain the leaves out, reserving the milk in a mug the child can use. Stir in the ashwagandha and cocoa powders, if using, and add the vanilla and honey. Cool just enough to drink, and serve warm.

Aromatics for the Respiratory System

Because they are expectorant, aromatic herbs are helpful in respiratory conditions. Bee balm, yarrow, and thyme are excellent herbs for acute and chronic bronchial illness, including cough, phlegm, and croupy congestion. Angelica, with its sweet green scent, is an excellent aromatic for both upper and lower congestion, including sinusitis, stuffy or runny nose, and lower (bronchial) congestion. These herbs all make good additions to external pastes, oils, or salves that you may want to rub on the chest to open the airways and improve breathing. Most over-the-counter vapor rubs contain menthol or other aromatic substances that, when breathed, open airways and clear breathing.

Think about cases when a person is nervous and having difficulty breathing. Perhaps a teenager is anxious, and the anxiety triggers an asthma-like attack. Aromatic herbs support both the nervous system and the respiratory system, making plants such as hyssop, lemon verbena, or peppermint good support herbs for both calming the teen and addressing the tightening airways. Similarly, these herbs are useful during a cold or the flu, when a person is coughing terribly and can't relax, or because the illness brings on worry and fear.

Use caution with expectorant herbs such as mother-wort and yarrow; most expectorants are too strong for pregnant mothers (because they can stimulate the uterus) and should be avoided during pregnancy.

Other aromatic herbs support the respiratory system not only by being expectorant but also by being astringent. Sage, for example, is a fragrant aromatic that is prized for its ability to astringe (dry up or tone) tissues. A wet, croupy cough with excessive phlegm will respond well to the astringent properties of sage, which also contributes antimicrobial action and can strengthen the body's process of fighting infection.

Get Well Sage Tea

Aromatic herbs make delicious teas—even sage, which has an exotic, green-tea-like flavor.

½ cup fresh (or ¼ cup dried) sage leaves

1 cup just-boiled water

Honey to taste

Harvest the sage leaves, shred them into a teacup, and pour just-boiled water over them, or make a pot using the ratio of 1 teaspoon per cup of hot water, plus an extra spoonful for the pot. A blend could include sage, peppermint, elderflower, or pleurisy root, or it could be a blend of other aromatic herbs, such as yarrow, bee balm, catnip, lemon balm, thyme, hyssop, and (the bitter herb) horehound.

Aromatics for the Digestive System

Aromatic herbs support healthy digestion, easing common symptoms such as gas, bloating, diarrhea, and constipation. Many digestive complaints respond positively to fragrant herbal remedies, which can be given as honeys, syrups, tinctures, teas, and powders mixed with juice.

Lemon balm is excellent for the person whose anxiety causes nausea; ginger supports the person whose fear leads to upset stomach; and tulsi, another aromatic with a fragrance similar to catnip, is a lovely nervine tonic that eases nervousness as well as irritable bowel issues. Motherwort is useful for those for whom nervous anxiety leads to poor digestion (as well as high blood pressure), and it can be used in a bitter remedy to be taken before and after meals. Angelica has been candied for hundreds of years and used to ease upset tummies, and aromatic fennel is a mother's mainstay for nausea both during pregnancy and during breastfeeding, when the baby has colic.

The trifecta is when someone is dealing with all three issues: anxiety or depression, along with troubled breathing and an upset stomach. This can happen for a variety of reasons: a cold can make someone's breathing congested, leading to postnasal drip, an upset stomach, and a cranky outlook. Or the nervous condition such as fear, panic, or grief can lead to shortness of breath and poor digestion. In both cases, aromatic herbs can provide relief and will support the person regaining a sense of both mental and physical stability.

Using Aromatics

Be creative in using these fragrant herbs. The best way is to chew on a fresh leaf and enjoy both the scent and the flavor. Often, this is enough to produce the desired effect.

If you'd like to create a remedy that is portable or shelf stable, consider the following ideas:

Syrup
Infuse 1 cup water with your chopped fresh or dried aromatic herb(s), and add ½ cup honey. Alternatively, infuse the honey with the herbs and add water. Infusing both the honey and the

water creates a strong remedy with a heady scent and flavor that is very enjoyable. Store the syrup in the refrigerator for up to a week.

Tincture

Use grain alcohol such as vodka or rum as the base for infusing aromatic herbs, especially cinnamon, cardamom, ginger, and yarrow. Because this is a concentrated form, only 25 drops is a dose; take 3–4 times daily. Store the tincture bottle in a pantry shelf or cabinet; it has a long shelf life, often years.

Tea

Lemon balm, bee balm, fennel, hyssop, thyme, sage, and angelica make lovely teas. Steep them 8–12 minutes, stir in honey if desired, and sip. A daily does is 3–4 cups. Yarrow and motherwort also make good teas, but they can become bitter quickly, so steep them for only a minute or two. Green tea with cinnamon and peppermint is a Moroccan traditional tea and is a wonderful way to enjoy these aromatic plants. Once you've brewed your tea, store any leftovers in the refrigerator and drink within a day. When I make hot teas, I like to brew an entire quart in the morning and store the tea in a thermos so it is ready to drink hot all day long. If you've made a blend of dried herbs, store them in a tightly closed tin or container in a dark cabinet for up to a year.

Salve

Topically, aromatic herbs provide warmth, stimulating blood flow and allowing the scent of the plant to be inhaled. All these herbs make good salve additions; use caution, as they can burn on sensitive skin. Some aromatics, such as yarrow and thyme, are healing first-aid herbs and deserve a place in your first-aid ointments. Store salves in a cool, dry place for up to two years.

Bath

Get out your largest pot and fill it with water about an hour before you plan to bathe. Shred any of the fresh aromatic leaves and flowers in the table on page 135 into the pot and let it steep until it is a strong tea. Dip yourself a cup from this pot and drink it if you like—it will be delicious. Place a large colander or pasta strainer in the bottom of the tub. Then, using hot mitts to protect your hands, pour the pot of water through the colander and continue filling the tub from the faucet. Enjoy soaking in this fragrant bath, which will open congested airways, ease the spirits, and soothe an upset stomach.

Herbal Bath Recipes

⇨ Vannoy Gentles Fite ⇦

Bathing with herbs is a practice as old as time. The properties released from the herbs into the tub can have so many beneficial effects. These herbs in the bath can touch all our senses with their beauty, healing, aromas, and overall mental effects. Each herb produces various effects on our skin and psyche, in ways that are often astounding. Bathing with herbs is such a sensual experience in itself, and the types of herbs that you incorporate can have effects on your emotions, ranging from aphrodisiacs to soothing anger to promoting energy to releasing worry!

Herbal Oils

There are boundless ways to incorporate herbs into your daily living routine and bathing rituals. The first is herbal oils. There is a multitude of ways that you can make yourself a bottle of herbal oil and even more ways to use it. This chapter will begin with a couple of recipes for the basics of making herbal oils. You can use these oils in beauty products, cooking, and medicines, and the uses are endless. The process can sometimes be time-consuming, but the oils can also be made quickly. Get started now on your herbal oils so you can have these oils handy for your future herbal needs.

The oils that you choose to use depend on how you want to use your herbal oil. For the recipes listed in this article, you will want to use oils that are good for your skin type. Some personal favorites are sesame oil and sweet almond oil for overall dry skin. You can use avocado oil, apricot oil, grape-seed oil, jojoba oil, and even olive oil. The types of oils are as varied as the herbs used to soak in them.

The herbs that you use to make your herbal oils depend on what you want out of your bathing rituals. Do you want energy-promoting herbal oil? Relaxing and calming oil? Stress-relieving oil? The possibilities are endless. Each herb offers various therapeutic properties that will be released into your bath. Read the recipes that follow to decide which herbs you wish to incorporate in making your herbal oils.

When using these herbs for your bath, you can interchange herbs. For example, if you don't want a calming sachet bath, then you can switch the melissa for a more energy-producing herb, such as a mint, tarragon, or ginseng. Or if you want a calming bath instead of an energizing bath, substitute the spearmint oil with valerian oil, rose oil, coriander oil, or green tea oil. The more you learn about herbs, the more you will be able to adapt recipes to suit your needs.

Remember, always pay attention to warnings associated with each herb. You may also want to do a small spot test of each herb or herbal oil on your skin before bathing with it.

Oil Infusion Methods

Long Infusion Herbal Oil Method

This is my favorite herbal oil method, but it takes time. You can use any herbs (as long as you know about the warnings for each herb beforehand) and just about any oil that you like. An herbal oil for bathing should contain herbs that either calm and relax you for evening bathing or energize and wake you for morning bathing. You'll need:

¾ cups herbs, chopped

1½ cups oil

Place the chopped herbs into a mason jar with a very tight-fitting lid. Pour enough oil into the container to cover the herbs. Place lid on jar and shake vigorously. Place the jar in a cool, dark area for at least 2 weeks, and you can leave it as long as 2 months. For the first 3 days, you will shake the jar to release the properties into the oil. After 3 days, leave the oil in a cool, dark area, until you are ready to decant. When the time is right for you, strain the oil through cheesecloth and discard the herbs into your compost. You can store your herbal oil in a cool, dark area for up to 1 year. This recipe yields 1½ cups.

You can use your oil in many bathing, cooking, and medicinal recipes. It just depends on which oils you decide to make.

Short Infusion Herbal Oil Method

Use this method if you are in a hurry to make your herbal oils. Many people disagree about which method is superior.

It's totally up to the herbalist which method is preferred. The therapeutic properties are attached to the oil either way. You'll need:

 1½ cups oil

 ¾ chopped herbs

Put oil in a glass or stainless-steel pan and heat on low. Add crushed herbs and stir. Lower heat to warm and let simmer for 1 hour. Cool completely. Strain the oil through cheesecloth, discard the herbs into compost, bottle the herbal oil, and label. Store in a cool, dark area in a jar with a tight-fitting lid for up to a year. This recipe yields 1½ cups.

Bath Recipes

Except for the bath salts, the following recipes all yield one application. Follow the oil infusion recipes given earlier to make the herbal oils listed in the ingredients.

Calming Melissa Bath Sachet

Calming ourselves down after an exhausting day can sometimes be easier said than done. Not only will taking a soothing bath relax our mental state, but it can also impart healthy benefits to our skin and our general overall health. Lemon balm (melissa) contains such therapeutic properties as antidepressant, antihistamine, antispasmodic, bactericidal, nervine, sedative, and sudorific. All these properties lend themselves to a bath that will relax, calm, and soothe us as well as clearing our respiratory system for a great night's sleep.

 1 6-inch square cheesecloth

 2 tablespoons lemon balm

 1 foot ribbon

Lay the cheesecloth flat on a table. Place the lemon balm directly into the center of the cloth. Pull up all the edges of the cloth to make a bag containing the herbs. Tie the ribbon close to the center of the gathered cloth to contain all the herbs so that they don't float in the tub. Before you get into the tub of not-too-hot water, gently squeeze the ball of herbs to release the properties of the herbs. Leave the herbs floating in the tub as long as you are bathing. When you are ready to leave the tub, discard the sachet into the compost.

Energizing Bath

The therapeutic properties of spearmint include restorative, stimulating, and tonic components. Spearmint is a natural fatigue reducer and can also alleviate stress. Taking a quick soak in a spearmint bath can help you get a great start to your day. Adding milk to the tub can help the oils disperse throughout the water. Try this recipe for an early morning bath to get your body and spirit in the positive, energizing frame of mind for the day.

1 tablespoon spearmint herbal oil

1 tablespoon milk

Once the tub is full of warm water, add the spearmint herbal oil and the milk. Relax in the tub as long as the water is comfortable. When you get out of the tub, be sure to dry your feet especially well, as the oils can cause your feet to be slippery. Enjoy your energized day.

Zen Foot Bath

Sometimes all you need is a quick foot bath to bring a sense of calm and peace to your overall well-being. These herbs provide calming, relaxing, and anti-inflammatory properties to your foot bath. Relax and let the zen take you away.

Water (enough to fill foot bath container ¾ full)

2 tablespoons chamomile, slightly crushed

2 tablespoons chickweed, slightly crushed

Heat the water as hot as you can stand it without scalding yourself. Pour the water into a container large enough for your feet. You can either place the herbs directly into the water or tie them up in a piece of linen and float it in the water. Place your feet in the water, sit back, and relax. Ten to 15 minutes is an ideal amount of time for the herbs to bring you contentment and peace. Discard the herbs and water once the footbath is completed.

Overall Skin Healing Soak

These herbs have skin-relieving agents, including emollients, anti-inflammatory, circulation-promoting, disinfecting, anti-fungal, and antibacterial properties. Soaking in a bath with these herbs can bring healing, great relief, overall glow, and softness to the skin. They feel and smell luxurious and make bathtime a private spa day. Choose the herbal oil from this list that you have on hand and this recipe is quick and easy.

1 tablespoon herbal oil: choose either rose petal, slippery elm, tarragon, agrimony, basil, burdock root, calendula, caraway, or fennel seed

1 tablespoon milk

Once the tub is full of warm water, add the oil of your choice and the milk. The milk helps disperse the herbal oil throughout the water and keeps it from adhering to your skin. Relax in the tub as long as the water is comfortable. When you get out of the tub, be sure to dry your feet especially well, as the oils can cause them to be slippery.

Sinus Opening Bath

Herbs are well known for their abilities to open the sinuses, relieve congestion, ease cough, and end headaches. The therapeutic properties inherent in these particular herbs are antibiotic, febrifuge, antiviral, anti-inflammatory, decongestant, expectorant, and mucolytic.

> 2 tablespoons herbal oil: 1 or 2 of eucalyptus, peppermint, chamomile, goldenseal, hibiscus, marjoram, or milk thistle
>
> 1 tablespoon milk

Once the tub is full of warm water, add the herbal oil of your choice and the milk. Relax in the tub as long as the water is comfortable. When you get out of the tub, be sure to dry your feet especially well, as the oils can cause them to be slippery.

Bath Sachet of Passion

Many herbs are considered to be aphrodisiacal in nature. These herbs contain therapeutic properties known to stimulate the sexual portion of a person's brain. Try this with your partner the next time you want to push the boundaries of passion in your life.

> 8-inch piece cheesecloth
>
> 1 tablespoon rose petals
>
> 1 teaspoon *Ginkgo biloba*
>
> 1½ inch piece ginger, grated
>
> 1 foot ribbon

Lay the cheesecloth flat on a table. Place the herbs directly into the center of the cloth. Pull up all the edges of the cloth to make a bag containing the herbs. Tie the ribbon close to the center of the gathered cloth to contain all the herbs so that they don't float in the tub. Before you get into the tub of not-too-hot water, gently squeeze the ball of herbs to release the properties of the herbs. Leave the herbs floating in the tub as long as you are bathing. When you are ready to leave the tub, discard the sachet into the compost.

Happy Joy Bath

Many herbs contain antidepressant properties. Soaking in a bath with these herbs can lift you out of that dark hole and bring some joy and passion back to your life. Some of the herbs with antidepressant properties that can increase the serotonin in the brain include St. John's wort, ginseng, chamomile, lavender, and saffron, reports registered nurse Nicole Galan for Medical News Today. Get a head start and make yourself a bottle of herbal oil containing one or more of these herbs.

> 2 tablespoons herbal oil: choose either St. John's wort, ginseng, chamomile, lavender, or saffron
>
> 1 tablespoon milk

Once the tub is full of warm water, add the herbal oil of your choice and the milk. The milk helps disperse the herbal oils throughout the water and keeps them from adhering to your skin. Relax in the tub as long as the water is comfortable. When you get out of the tub, be sure to dry your feet especially well, as the oils can cause them to be slippery.

Herbal Bath Salts

Bath salts can be either energizing or calming, depending on the type of herbal oil you choose to use. Use lemon balm, rose, or chamomile herbal oil for calming. If you want an energy-filled bath, use mint, nettle, or dandelion herbal oil.

3 tablespoons herbal oil

3 cups salt, any type (pink Himalayan salt, sea salt, Epsom salt, etc.)

1 tablespoon milk

In a small container, add the herbal oils to the desired type of salt. Stir until herbal oil and salt mixture is well blended. Screw lid onto container tightly. Leave mixture in a dark area for 24 hours, and then stir mixture again.

Run a lukewarm bath. After the tub is full of water, you can add the milk. Add ½ cup of the bath salt mixture to bathwater as you get into the tub.

Store the remainder in a glass jar or a container with a tight-fitting lid in a cool, dark area for up to 3 months. Jars of herbal bath salts make attractive, inexpensive, and healing gifts!

Invite Herbs into Your Life

Experiment with all these recipes, fine-tune them to meet your needs, and keep trying to use new herbs in different ways. Learn the therapeutic properties of herbs and how you can treat your various cleaning, culinary, health, or aromatic needs with them. You can utilize the healing benefits of herbs for every ailment—physical, mental, or spiritual—that you can think of. Getting educated about herbs and their uses can help make you a natural healer for everyone you know.

Herbal oils, bath sachets, and herbal bath salts make great gifts. Every time you make an herbal product, double or triple it so that you can have gifts on hand for others. You can also make decoctions, tinctures, herbal spice mixes, syrups, oils, balms, salves, rubs, teas, ointments and hundreds of other medicinal or culinary gifts.

Herbs can last for a long time if stored properly. Make sure your herbs are in an airtight container and out of the reach of children. Storing them in a cool, dark area is best. They can be kept in mason jars with tight lids, in ziplock bags, or in any container that won't let moisture, mold, or mildew inside.

Incorporate herbs into your daily life by experimenting with fresh herbs for cooking, drinking teas made from herbs you grow in your own patio garden, making salves and ointments from herbs, and using your dried herbs as a base for creative gifts.

Growing your own herbs is one of the most rewarding hobbies you can have. It just takes a little pot with some soil in it and some sunshine. Most herbs don't require much watering and are easy to grow and multiply. Soon you will begin giving offshoots and cuttings to your friends, and they will, in turn, become herbalists too.

When you begin inviting herbs into your life, you will discover so many new ways to share and use herbs with others. When friends visit my home, we drink an energizing herbal tea. Then we go out to the garden where I let them harvest their own mint, parsley, thyme, rosemary, basil, or whatever herb I have on hand at that time of year. We then make a nice salad and have lunch using the fresh herbs we have just picked. When they leave my home, I gift them with a small bag of herbal oil bath salts or some dried sprigs of lavender tied with a bow. Needless to say, friends love visiting!

The most important thing is to keep learning, keep using, and keep spreading your knowledge of herbs. Teach the children what you know, and they will teach their own children. Respect herbal warnings and keep striving to learn.

Resource

Galan, Nicole. "8 Herbs and Supplements for Depression." Medical News Today. Last modified February 26, 2019. https://www.medicalnewstoday.com/articles/314421.

Making Medicine: Folk and Standard Herbal Tincture Methods

⤳ Monica Crosson ⤳

Imagine yourself walking down a country lane. Just beyond the hedgerow where the elderberry and blackberry intertwine with the wild rose, you may have, at one time, spied the old cunning man taking from his plant allies a bit of leaf or a few berries. He knew exactly the amount he needed, never taking more and always thanking them in his own way. Or maybe, as you wandered down a forested path, you might have stumbled upon the wise woman. She's the one who clucked her tongue as she ground the herbs that would become a powerful medicine when winter approached with sickness on its cold breath.

Before modern medicine, it was the cunning folk who were sought

after by the local community and revered for their knowledge. It was in their homes under the glow of firelight where poultices were made to help mend broken bones and promote healing or a special decoction was brewed to ease the melancholy caused by a broken heart. They were the healers who were there to create comfort and safety when a birth occurred and were also there to ease the dying as they took their last breath.

The folk healers of old may have been unfamiliar with the conventions of scholastic medical teachings, but they developed a high level of practical knowledge by making use of the wild plants of their regions and of the herbs, flowers, and shrubs they grew in their own gardens. Though today we may find their folkways quaint, it is evident that many people had a surprisingly sophisticated understanding of plant medicine.

Is It an Infusion, a Tincture, or a Decoction?

There is absolutely no doubt that modern medicine can offer an unparalleled opportunity to save lives, but it is also clear that herbal medicine has much to offer. The use of herbs in decoctions, infusions, teas, capsules, salves, and tinctures can complement conventional treatments and provide safe, well-tolerated remedies for many chronic conditions.

Medicinal herbs have been made into an extraordinary variety of formulas, from the simple cup of tea to the trickier herbal distillations, but in my own herbal dabblings, I've found tincturing particularly intriguing. Tincturing finds its roots mainly in the early medicinal practices of Europe, America, and Australia, but it has also played a role in most herbal traditions. But what exactly is a tincture, and how does it differ from an infusion or a decoction?

Infusions and decoctions are both forms of herbal extraction that use water as a menstruum (solvent). **Infusions** are similar to tea in that they typically use the aerial parts of the plant (especially leaves and flowers) that are steeped in boiling water and consumed in quantities of up to six cups per day. The difference between the two is that an infusion uses a greater amount of the herb and is steeped longer. Because bark, roots, twigs, and berries require a more forceful treatment, they can be simmered in hot water for up to thirty minutes to produce a highly concentrated liquid known as a **decoction**.

A **tincture** is basically a concentrated herbal extract that uses high-proof alcohol as a menstruum. Tinctures can be made with fresh or dried flowers, leaves, roots, berries, or resins and can have a shelf life of up to two years or more depending on conditions. They are usually taken internally by mouth. The easiest and most effective way is by putting your dosage (typically a few drops) into a couple of ounces of water and drinking it.

Gathering Your Herbs

Let's go back to the edge of the forest for just a few moments. Our cunning man is there taking elderflowers (just a few) from the elderberry whose branches wave slightly in the breeze. He has visited this area every spring since he was just a child and knows the uses for every plant. We know the tree he gathers from as elderberry or *Sambucus cerulea*, but he calls her by another folk name, Elder Mother, for the spirit of the tree that he believes resides within. He knows his plant allies well, not only by sight but by the scent they release as they prepare to bloom and by the flight patterns of birds as nuts and berries drop in the autumn. The wise women and cunning men followed the rhythms of the seasons and demonstrated an intimate knowledge of and respect for the flora that grew in their region.

For a balanced immune system and to help fight colds and flu, try making an elderberry tincture with the added antiviral properties of lemon balm and thyme.

Today, there are not that many of us living as closely with the land as our ancestors did and for people new to herbalism, our knowledge may be especially limited. So before planning which herbs you will use in making your herbal tinctures, let's consider a few things:

Your Herbal Needs
The types of herbs you will need will depend on what your herbal medicinal needs are. Do you want something for overall general health? How about something to induce a restful sleep or to relieve stress? Maybe you just need a little something to ease your digestion. This is the time to do a little research and make a list of the herbs best suited for your needs. Keep it simple by choosing plants that are easily identifiable—maybe they are already growing in your garden. Herbs like garlic, peppermint, and lavender are powerful plant allies that most people know and are easily attainable.

Local Sources

If you plan to purchase herbs for tinctures, before hitting the internet for your herbal needs, visit a trusted local herbalist. This way you know you are getting the freshest herbs that have been harvested ethically, and you're helping support a small local business.

Finding a Mentor

If you are interested in wildcrafting, seek out a knowledge-able herbal guide in your area to show you what to look for when foraging and proper foraging etiquette. Many areas offer classes.

Identification of Poisonous Plants

Know which plants are poisonous and how to treat affected areas if you come in contact with one.

Which Parts of the Plants to Use

I can't stress hard enough how important it is to know your plants. Different plant parts can have different constituents. You might be able to use the berries on one tree but the bark may be toxic. If you are not sure of a plant, don't take from it. Instead, take a photo of it and take it to a well-trusted herbalist or Master Gardener to help you identify it.

Responsible Harvesting

This goes back to finding a mentor. Before trudging into the forest with a shovel and a bag, ready to snatch up everything around you, find a guide who can teach you proper forging techniques. Remember these plants are our allies and we need to treat them with respect. A rule of thumb is to take only what you need and never more than one-third of the plant.

Using Your Weeds

Many common backyard weeds have medicinal uses. Try prolific plants such as dandelion or self-heal. Just remember to never take plant material from an area that may have been sprayed with pesticides or chemicals (such as roadways).

Growing Your Own

The benefit of growing your own herbs is that you know exactly what the plant is and what went into growing it. Having a small garden of herbal allies allows you to connect with the plants. By watching their seasonal changes and working with them hands on, this gives you an intimate connection to the spirit of the plant. Growing your own also gives you a better understanding of common wild plants. Consider St. John's wort, which is common both in herbal gardens and in the wild. If you're growing it, you will definitely know it when you see it in the wild.

Your Local Grocery Store

So you don't have a lot of time for foraging or gardening—I get it. A lot of herbs and spices that can be tinctured can be found in your local grocery store or are already sitting on a shelf in your pantry. Cinnamon sticks, turmeric, ginger root, and cayenne are just a few of the commonly found grocery items that can be used in tincturing.

Common Herbs

In this table, I have provided a list of common herbs for tinctures and their uses:

Plant	Botanical Name	Uses in Tincture
Burdock	*Arctium lappa*	Eases arthritis, cleanses the body of toxins, is antiseptic
Calendula	*Calendula officinalis*	Promotes natural healing
Cayenne	*Capsicum annuum*	May help ease pain from arthritis, increases blood flow, is a warming stimulant
Chamomile	*Matricaria chamomilla*	Promotes a restful sleep, eases anxiety
Cinnamon	*Cinnamomum verum*	Cold and flu prevention, eases digestive problems
Dandelion	*Taraxacum officinale*	Relieves heartburn, reduces cholesterol, supports healthy liver and kidney function, reduces inflamation
Echinacea	*Echinacea angustifolia*	Helps prevent cold and flu and boosts immune system
Elderberry	*Sambucus nigra* *Sambucus cerulea*	Use flowers and berries for cold and flu prevention, supports immune system
Feverfew	*Tanacetum parthenium*	Eases migraines or head-aches, may reduce the effects of arthritis
Garlic	*Allium sativum*	Helps with circulatory disorders, may lower blood pressure, has antibiotic properties
Ginger	*Zingiber officinale*	Reduces inflammation, relieves digestive problems, has antibacterial properties

Plant	Botanical Name	Uses in Tincture
Goldenseal	*Hydrastis canadensis*	Reduces excess mucus, is astringent, eases inflammation
Hawthorn	*Crataegus monogyna*	Increases blood flow, restoring heartbeat
Lavender	*Lavandula officinalis*	Promotes restful sleep and stress relief
Lemon balm	*Melissa officinalis*	Eases anxiety and depression, aids sleep
Mullein	*Verbascum thapsus*	Helps relieve cough and congestion, reduces mucus, and stimulates coughing up phlegm
Nettle	*Urtica dioica*	Is nutritious and high in vitamins and minerals, increases flow of breast milk
Peppermint	*Mentha ×piperita*	Eases digestion and other common stomach ailments
Raspberry leaf	*Rubus idaeus*	Supports pregnancy and menstrual cramps, helps prevent cold and flu
Rosemary	*Rosmarinus officinalis*	Has antibacterial properties, relieves stress
Sage	*Salvia officinalis*	Regulates menstruation, eases digestion, relieves sore throat
St. John's wort	*Hypericum perforatum*	Eases anxiety and depression, relieves inflammation

Plant	Botanical Name	Uses in Tincture
Self-heal	*Prunella vulgaris*	Eases bleeding gums as a mouthwash, may reduce blood pressure, relieves sore throat
Skullcap	*Scutellaria lateriflora*	Reduces stress, helps promote restful sleep
Thyme	*Thymus vulgaris*	Eases respiratory tract, soothes cough or sore throat, relieves muscle spasms
Turmeric	*Curcuma longa*	May help lower cholesterol, eases stomach pain, is anti-inflammatory
Valerian	*Valeriana officinalis*	Reduces nervous tension, is a relaxant, promotes restful sleep
Willow	*Salix alba*	Reduces fever, is anti-inflammatory
Yarrow	*Achillea millefolium*	Reduces fever, may lower blood pressure, prevents cold and flu

Time to Tincture

Unlike an infusion or a decoction, tinctures take longer to make—anywhere from a couple of weeks to a couple of months to fully saturate the liquid with the plant medicine—but they're worth it. By using ethanol alcohol as a menstruum, the extraction of the beneficial medicinal qualities is generally more concentrated than in water extracts. Because of this concentration, tinctures may also be faster acting than water extracts, and they can maintain their potency for a long time.

The Folk Method

This is how the folk healers of a bygone time would have made their own tinctures and how many experienced herbalists make their own tinctures today. It is simple and practical and doesn't require a scale or any real math skills. If you consider yourself an "intuitive" herbalist, this is the only way to go. The downside is this method does not provide the consistency of the modern standard method, which may affect dosing. You will need:

Plant material (dried or fresh):

> For fresh leaves and flowers, enough chopped fresh herbs to fill a pint jar ¾ full (lightly packed)
>
> For dried herbs, enough dried herbs to fill approximately half of the jar
>
> For dried roots, barks, and berries, enough finely cut material to fill ¼ to ⅓ of pint jar

Wide-mouth pint jar with lid

100-proof vodka or grain alcohol

Cheesecloth

Amber tincture bottles with glass pipettes (available online)

Chop your fresh herbs or grind your dried herbs. If using fresh herbs, lightly pack your jar to approximately ¾ full. If using dried herbs, fill approximately half the jar. If using bark, roots, or berries, fill approximately ¼ to ⅓ of the jar. Pour your menstruum over the herbs to the top of the jar (cover plant material completely) and secure the lid. Shake well. Label your jar with the name of the plant (botanical and common) and the date. Set it aside in a warm place and shake once daily for 4–6 weeks. Using the cheesecloth, strain the liquid and transfer to amber glass jars. Store in a cool, dark place.

The Standard Method

If you want to produce a product that yields the same effectiveness each and every time, then the standard method of tincturing is for you. Using this method takes the guesswork out of your tincture making. If you plan on selling your products and are worried about consistency, use this method. The downside is this method does not allow for much flexibility. You must be consistent in terms of volume, weight, and percentage of alcohol in order for it to work. Follow the ratios in the next section to get your amounts for this method. You will need:

  Plant material (dried or fresh)

  Kitchen scale

  Wide-mouth glass jar with lid

  High-proof vodka or grain alcohol

  Water (depending on preparation and ratio)

  Cheesecloth

  Amber tincture bottles with glass pipettes (available
      online)

Chop your fresh herbs or grind your dried herbs. Using your kitchen scale, measure your herbs by weight (ounces or grams) and place them in the jar. Measure out the correct volume of menstruum (ounces or milliliters). Pour your menstruum over the herbs and secure the lid. Shake well. Label your jar with the name of the plant (botanical and common) and the date. Set aside in a warm place and shake once daily for 4–6 weeks. Using the cheesecloth, strain the liquid and transfer to amber glass jars. Store in a cool, dark place.

Basic Weight-to-Volume Ratios

There are three important numbers used when figuring out your tincture preparation:

1. Plant material weight
2. Menstruum volume
3. Percentage of alcohol you are starting with

Alcohol percentages can be easily figured out by dividing the proof in half. So, if you have 100-proof vodka, divide that in half to get 50. If you subtract this number from 100, this will tell you the percentage of water: 100 − 50 = 50. Therefore, 100-proof vodka is 50 percent alcohol and 50 percent water.

Any proof will work for tincturing. If you have a 190-proof alcohol, it can be used for many different tinctures by diluting it down instead of buying varying bottles at different percents.

Fresh plant to menstruum volume ratio: 1:2 (with 95 percent alcohol content)

For example, you have 5 ounces of fresh raspberry leaves and 190-proof grain alcohol. The math would look like this:

190 divided in half is 95 percent alcohol content (we do not need to dilute our menstruum).

5 ounces of herb with a 1:2 ratio is 5 × 2 = 10.

Your ratio is 5:10. This means 5 ounces of raspberry leaves in 10 ounces of 95 percent alcohol.

Dried plant to menstruum volume ratio: 1:5 (with 50–65 percent alcohol content)

For example, you have 8 ounces of dried lavender that you want to tincture in 60 percent ethanol at the standard ratio of 1:5, and you have 190-proof grain alcohol (95 percent alcohol content). This is what the math would look like:

8 ounces of herb with 1:5 ratio is 8 × 5 = 40.

Menstruum will be 40 ounces of 60 percent ethanol.

Change your 95 percent ethanol to 60 percent by dividing 95 by 60, which equals 1.58.

Divide how many ounces of menstruum you need (40) by the number above (1.58): 40 / 1.58 = 25.3.

You will need 25.3 ounces of 95 percent alcohol.

To figure out the amount of water needed to dilute the alcohol, subtract 25.3 (ounces of 95 percent alcohol) from the total amount of menstruum needed (40 ounces): 40 − 25.3 = 14.7.

This means 25.3 ounces of 95 percent alcohol and 14.7 ounces of water will give you a 60 percent alcohol content.

Further Reading

Chevallier, Andrew. *The Encyclopedia of Medicinal Plants*. London: Dorling Kindersley, 1996.

Gladstar, Rosemary. *Rosemary Gladstar's Medicinal Herbs: A Beginner's Guide*. North Adams, MA: Storey Publishing, 2012.

How to Make Your Own Herbal Chewables

❧ Kristen Schuhmann ☙

B ack in high school when I first started getting interested in herbs, I used to go to my local natural foods store and spend all my time perusing their extensive bulk herb section. I loved unscrewing the tops of those glass containers and pouring dried nettles, peppermint, and exotic-sounding herbs such as *dong quai* into little baggies to take home. The smell was intoxicating, and I felt closer to understanding the herbs in that way, where they were loose and free, instead of in a closed-up pill bottle or tincture. Once I got them home, if I didn't want to drink the herbs as a tisane, I would spend hours scooping the powdered herbs into gelatin capsules that I'd also gotten from the bulk section of that natural foods store. It was a time-consuming task, but I enjoyed getting to know each herb intimately as I filled capsules. Something about working with those wild beauties sparked a lifelong love affair with all sorts of herbal crafting and concocting.

As I got older and life got busier, I stopped filling my own capsules, and although I enjoyed making tinctures and oils and crafting with herbs in other ways, I never took the time to go back to filling those little gel caps. Eventually, I did return to powdered herbs, though, when I started boosting my smoothies, teas, and coffees with herbal blends. When using the whole herb as a powder, you get the all the benefits of the whole herb without any fillers or additives, which means all the fiber, vitamins, minerals, and other nutritious components are there, with no alcohol, glycerin, or gelatin added to it. The powders are pure and potent and can be blended together to create synergistic combinations. I like to make blends that are immune boosters and digestives, which go into my sons' smoothies, and I take digestives and adaptogens in my drinks all day long.

I then learned how to make these powders into chewable pills, which could also be dropped into hot drinks and taken that way, and this brought me full circle to my introduction into herbal crafting. This time the herbs were not locked away in a gel capsule; instead they were simply mixed with an edible and medicinal binder, then popped right into one's mouth or beverage to be enjoyed. It is far less time-consuming than filling gel caps and a healthier, more enjoyable way to take the herbs.

The actual taste of herbs is often an important component in its healing work, especially bitters. Tisanes and tinctures are great for tasting herbs, but pills are generally a little bit less about the taste and more about easy delivery. Chewables, on the other hand, are all about tasting the herb as well as easy delivery, plus you get the herb in its entirety, not just the water-soluble or alcohol-soluble components. The binder can be honey, agave nectar, ghee, or coconut oil, depending on taste, what you are trying to accomplish, and how you intend to take the chewables. If you plan on dropping them into tea or hot water, then honey or agave nectar might be desired; if you are addressing digestive issues, ghee might be preferred; or if you like coconut oil in your coffee, that might be the binder of choice for some. This is one of the best benefits of crafting your own herbal medicine in any form—you get to create a custom blend that is specific to your or your loved ones' own unique needs and desires.

How to Make Herbal Chewables

To make these "chewables," which actually can be chewed, sucked on like a lozenge, or put into a hot drink, start with powdered herbs. If you don't have powdered herbs handy, simply use an old coffee grinder or food processor to powder dry herbs. You can also use a mortar and pestle, of course—just make sure the herbs are ground up really well so the digestive system has the best chance of getting all the nutrition out of them.

Once you have your herbs powdered, place them in a bowl and add honey, agave nectar, coconut oil, or ghee to the herbs, a little bit at a time, until the mixture is roughly the consistency of cream cheese. If using ghee or coconut oil, warm it first on a stove top, then add it to the herbs.

Ghee is a great choice for digestibility of the herbs, but honey and agave nectar offer their own benefits as well. Honey, if local, can help with allergies and is soothing to the throat. Agave nectar has less of an effect on the glycemic index so can be added for sweetness without as much sugar spike as honey. Coconut oil is another option, and it too has a host of benefits of its own. Many people use it for a variety of reasons, from weight management to immune boosting.

You will want to have a glass container ready, preferably lined with wax paper. Once the mixture is fully blended together, take a teaspoon of the blend and roll into a ball with clean hands, then place in the container. It can be helpful to have some of the dry powdered herbs in a separate container to roll the mixture in so the outside of the balls is coated with the herbs. This helps the balls form more easily, but it isn't necessary to do. When all the balls are formed, put them in the refrigerator for at least three hours or overnight to let them fully set. They will still be malleable and somewhat sticky, so they are not ever intended to be swallowed whole. These are for chewing or for dissolving into hot beverages only.

About one tablespoon per day (three teaspoons) is appropriate for most people and conditions, but always consult your health care provider and a trusted natural health practitioner for more personal instructions.

To increase the effectiveness of herbal blends, add a small blend of ginger or black pepper to support the transport and bioavailability of the herbs throughout the body. Just be sure to keep the amount fairly low to ensure the chewables aren't too spicy.

Choose the herbs and binders that work best for you, but here are a few recipes to get you started. Feel free to increase the yield of the recipes, but keep in mind these should really be used within a week for highest potency, although they will keep in a refrigerator for up to three months.

Bitter Chewable

Bitters are a class of herbs that really need to be tasted in order to work. They help get the digestive system off to a great start by encouraging the activation of the body's natural enzymes, among other things. Gentian root is a well-known bitter that can be combined with other herbs or used alone for a bitter start to a meal. (That's a good thing!)

1 tablespoon gentian root powder

1 teaspoon cardamom powder

1 teaspoon licorice root powder

Enough agave nectar to make a paste, about 1 tablespoon

Mix the ingredients together with a wooden chopstick and roll into small, 1-teaspoon sized balls. Roll the balls into additional dry, powdered herbs, if using. Refrigerate. Makes approximately 6 chewables.

Take 1 before each meal either in a hot drink or just by chewing.

Digestive Chewable

This is a fairly spicy combination that encourages proper digestion and nutrient absorption. This mix is also anti-inflammatory and full of antioxidants. You can replace the cacao powder with turmeric to make it even more anti-inflammatory, but remember, turmeric stains, so be careful to not get it on your clothing or counters. I like the cacao in there because it has so many antioxidants, and the depth of flavor it adds is appealing.

1 tablespoon cinnamon powder

1 tablespoon ginger powder

1 tablespoon cacao powder

1 teaspoon cardamom powder

½ teaspoon clove powder

½ teaspoon nutmeg powder

A couple of turns of freshly ground black pepper

Enough local honey to make a paste, about 3½ tablespoons

Mix the ingredients together with a wooden chopstick and roll into small, 1-teaspoon sized balls. Roll the balls into additional dry, powdered herbs, if using. Refrigerate. Makes approximately 12 chewables.

Take 1 before or after each meal either in a hot drink or just by chewing. These are especially good in black tea because they are a quick way to make a chai. If chewing on this combination, be ready for a spicy bite.

Adaptogenic Chewable

Adaptogens are herbs that help us handle all kinds of stress, such as emotional, physical, environmental, and mental. It is no wonder this classification of herbs has become so popular in these fast-paced modern times. Because adaptogens work through the endocrine system, which is the home and regulatory system for our hormones, and our hormones are responsible for sending messages to our entire body, it is easy to see how adaptogens effect every single aspect of our body as a whole, including the immune system and mental health.

The herbs in this recipe are deeply penetrating, which means they have to be taken consistently over time to get the best results. Luckily for us, some are tasty enough to eat and drink all day long.

1 tablespoon tulsi powder (also called holy basil)

1 tablespoon eleuthero powder

1 tablespoon rhodiola powder

1 teaspoon licorice root powder

Enough ghee to make a paste, a little over 3 tablespoons of ghee

Mix the ingredients together with a wooden chopstick and roll into balls about 1 teaspoon each in size. Roll into dry powdered herbs if using, refrigerate, then take throughout the day between or with meals. Makes approximately 10 chewables.

Take up to 3 teaspoon-size balls per day. I actually like the taste of these adaptogens, but they may not be everybody's cup of tea. You can always increase the licorice root for more sweetness or leave out any herb that just doesn't tickle your taste buds. If you aren't familiar with the tastes of these herbs, start with the tulsi because it is mild, grassy, and pleasant to most people.

Immune System Chewable

One of my herb teachers used to always talk about how in China all the grandmothers knew to put strips of astragalus root into their soups all winter long to keep their families well. I can't confirm the truth of that today, but astragalus has certainly had a long tradition of being an immunomodulator in both Traditional Chinese Medicine and Ayurvedic traditions. This means that if your immune system needs a boost, it will boost, but if your immune system is overzealous (think allergies or rheumatoid arthritis), astragalus can help moderate it. This is different from the common cold and flu herb, echinacea, which is a good immune booster, but after you are feeling better, you need to stop taking it or else it loses efficacy for you. Astragalus, on the other hand, can be taken all winter long, and it will help keep your immune system pitch-perfect. It also has adaptogenic properties as well, which is a bonus.

3 tablespoons astragalus powder

1 teaspoon licorice root powder

Enough honey to make a paste, a little over 3 tablespoons Mix the ingredients together with a wooden chopstick and roll into small, 1-teaspoon sized balls. Roll the balls into additional dry, powdered herbs, if using. Refrigerate. Makes approximately 10 chewables.

Use up to 3 per day. If you intend to put this into soup, use ghee or coconut oil instead of the honey, and leave out the licorice if you prefer. The licorice just provides a bit of sweetness and has adaptogenic properties of its own. Again, I like the taste of astragulus, which is somewhat nutty, but you can always increase the licorice if you need to balance out the taste more.

A Note on Licorice

Two recipes in this article use licorice. Licorice has been shown to raise blood pressure when taken in large amounts with long-term use. Although licorice has long been one of the top-ten most used herbs in TCM and has been added in small amounts to preparations for centuries, it is best to avoid if pregnant or if you have high blood pressure.

Herbal Body Scrubs

≫ Divina Cornick ≪

The skin is our largest organ. I never really understood that until I started battling acne in my mid-twenties. I caked on as many miracle products as I could buy, thinking one of them would have to deliver what its label promised. A few worked, to an extent, but for the most part my skin rebelled terribly, dried out, and broke out worse than before.

One day, my German Shepherd, who was still a young, floppy puppy, wormed herself into the bathroom and got a hold of one of those face moisturizers. Thankfully, she has a proud personality and proceeded to parade her find around the house. I lunged and grabbed it out of her mouth, yelling something like "Don't eat that—you could die!"

It was a bit of a lightbulb moment.

All the products on my bathroom counter contained labels warning against ingesting them. "Call poison control if swallowed"—things like that. Anything you put on your skin is absorbed into said skin. We often buy chemical-packed products because of their absorbent qualities. We want our skin soft and healthy, vibrant and glowing! I think I assumed that because I was putting something on my skin, it wasn't going in me. It's for topical, external uses only, right? But, if it's being absorbed, that means it's going internal, to an extent.

Ew. I threw out so much stuff. It felt like I set my paycheck on fire, but I threw all the creams, lotions, masks, and scrubs into the trash. Kris Carr, who is healing her cancer from the inside out through diet and lifestyle changes, wrote in *Crazy Sexy Cancer Survivor* that "if it's invented in a laboratory, it'll take a laboratory to digest." Now, you don't really want to eat any of these for lunch. When you hear "don't put anything on your skin that you wouldn't put in your mouth," this means the ingredients. You can eat salt, coconut oil, peppermint, and so on, but you don't really want to eat a whole handful of salt at once—health-wise or taste-wise.

I use sea salt and coconut oil in all my scrubs. Sea salt is cleansing and adds that coarse and gritty texture we all crave in a scrub. Coconut oil is an amazing all-natural moisturizer that has more uses than you can imagine, including cleansing. If you're allergic to or simply don't like the smell of coconut oil, you can use grapeseed oil or argan oil instead.

I don't often have leftovers when I make the following recipes, as I use a generous amount of the scrubs. However, if you want to make a large amount to use at your leisure, store them in a cool and dry place in a glass jar or ziplock bag for one week.

Keep in mind that if you are using coconut oil, the scrub will harden in a cool environment. Be sure to stir up the ingredients again to loosen up the coconut oil. If you are using grapeseed or argan oils, the same rules apply. They will not harden like the coconut oil, but the oils will pool together. Stir, stir, stir!

Here are a few of my go-to natural beauty recipes:

Luminous Body Scrub

This one does come with a warning label, though not the one that usually accompanies a beauty product. I'm trying to save you from having to do more laundry!

The gold turmeric will stain clothing. The best time to use this scrub is in the tub so you can clean the porcelain if needed. I recommend sitting in the tub on a towel you don't care too much about while you apply the scrub. You can also use the scrub in an actual bath, just be aware that the water will turn yellow and could stain the actual tub if it soaks for too long.

Also be sure to follow up the scrub with a good cleansing. I suggest coconut oil and some salt with warm water to wash away any coloring left behind on your skin.

Now for the fun part! You'll need:

1 cup sea salt

As much coconut oil as you like: use less for a coarse scrub and more for a softer scrub

1 teaspoon turmeric powder

1 tablespoon minced ginger

A few pinches cinnamon

When you have all the ingredients ready, simply mix them together. Use more of the dry ingredients for a dryer, coarse scrub or more oils for a smoother texture. To apply, you can rub it over your skin with your hands or you can purchase a bath glove or brush to really work the scrubs into your skin.

You can use this scrub anytime, but it's great in the summer. Your skin might not be dry, but it needs healing from the sun and other damage. This scrub will give you some added moisture and love.

This scrub is warming and great for dull skin. Add more coconut oil to the scrub if you want to use it on your face, but a coarser or harder scrub is ideal for the body. Of course, it's all about your preference. There's no right or wrong way to mix these scrubs.

The turmeric has anti-inflammatory properties and will target any scarred or upset skin. Ginger soothes redness and spots on the skin. Cinnamon has antifungal, antioxidant, and anti-inflammatory properties. Keep in mind, though, that cinnamon can be a tricky monster. It does dry out skin on its own, which is why the coconut oil is key!

Wake Me Up Face Scrub

Sometimes my job has me waking up at four o'clock in the morning. It can definitely be a struggle to get up that early, especially when I have a snuggly puppy in my bed and the mornings are cold.

This scrub is my favorite. It's a great addition to my morning routine, and I love this scrub for a lot of reasons, especially the smell. It's meant to wake you up and brighten your skin. I hope that it also brightens your day.

- 1 cup sea salt
- 1 tablespoon coffee grounds
- 4 tablespoons coconut oil

Ground mint leaves (preferably fresh leaves ground by
hand or mortar and pestle)

Squeeze of fresh orange or tangerine

Mix all the ingredients together with your hands. Start with 4
tablespoons of coconut oil and go from there, depending on
your preference. You want this scrub to be soft, almost runny, so
it's kind to the sensitive skin of your face. Massage your fingers
and palms with the scrub before gently rubbing it onto your
already damp face. Move it in small circles. Rinse clean when
you're done.

Coffee is high in antioxidants and protects your skin
against free radicals. Mint is an amazing herb to hydrate your
skin, especially when fresh. Orange has a high amount of cit-
ric acid. It can dry out the skin but can help clear away acne.

*I use Scandinavian coffee for this face scrub because
I'm in love with their practice of* fika. *It's roughly
translated as a break from work with coffee and a
pastry, but it is so much more on a spiritual level.*

Tough Love Body Scrub

This is primarily for places that need some extra love, like elbows and feet. It's a little harsher, so I don't recommend using
it on your face. The ingredients are usually associated with
relaxation and healing, but remember to keep the salt ratio
higher so it's a thick scrub.

2 cups sea salt

4 tablespoons coconut oil

½ cup rose petals

½ cup dried lavender

Rub it all over, paying attention to the areas of the body that get rough and dry, like elbows, knees, and feet.

I often jump in the shower after using this scrub to rinse it all off under hot water. Sometimes it's nice to rub more coconut oil on your skin so it absorbs.

Rose is perfect for exfoliating your skin and giving it extra moisture. Lavender will make your skin soft and smooth because of the antioxidants.

Nourish Your Skin

My acne flared up because of too much stress and a change in my hormones. I was visiting too many drive-throughs and not staying properly hydrated. There are too many reasons to list why your skin is being difficult. Always consult your health care provider if you feel something is wrong. Have a conversation with them about your needs and concerns. Ask them about healthy and holistic alternatives if you're not comfortable with certain medications. Trust your intuition, but always be open to the wise words of professionals. They are there to help you.

My acne cleared up once I started taking care of my body as a whole instead of applying products like bandages. You are so much more than the pimple on your chin. And don't just use these scrubs for emergency pimple relief. Stress is unfortunately a part of life. Use these scrubs before you need them, to cleanse and nourish the skin. Use them simply to do something nice for yourself. Add some luxury to your wellness routine.

Resource

Carr, Kris. *Crazy Sexy Cancer Survivor.* Guilford, CT: skirt!, 2008. Page 126.

DIY
and
Crafts

Garden Tech

∗ JD Hortwort ∗

When I talk to people about my childhood growing up in the foothills of North Carolina, I frequently spin tales about growing our own food and raising pigs and chickens. The first response is often "Well, that's nice. You come from a family of farmers."

We didn't farm. Farmers (at least where I lived) had big tractors and barns. They worked large pastures and fields, sometimes hundreds of acres. They grew crops or livestock to sell on the open market. We gardened—intensely. That's because my parents and grandmother counted on the food we raised to feed the family.

That meant everyone pitched in. For the younger kids, it meant watering, pulling weeds, and tossing rocks out of the half-acre garden plots Grandma had set up in three different spots around our homes. I still remember struggling to carry a five-gallon bucket of water into the tomato patch, sloshing more on the ground on the way to the garden than I distributed among the plants. I stopped at each plant to ladle out water, using a battered old pot that had seen better days in the kitchen.

"Why can't we use the hose, Grandma?" I would whine.

"You waste too much water," she said firmly. Grandma always seemed to be worried about running our well dry. Since I had no concept of family budgets and the cost to drill a new well, it never made sense to me.

My sisters and most of my brothers grew up with a definite distaste for gardening. They still prefer to pick their tomatoes and squash from a shelf, not a vine sprawling out under a blazing summer sun.

Over the years, memories of the suffering in the garden patch that I imagined Grandma, Mama, and Daddy inflicted on me in my youth have faded. As long as I have lived in a place with even a small plot of land, I have gardened. That doesn't mean I relish the chores of watering, weeding, and pest control.

Great Expectations

Let's face it. When people say they like gardening, they usually mean that they enjoy the satisfaction of seeing baby plants mature to full growth. They like the taste of fresh food and the heartwarming sense of knowing their bowl of salad or plate of grilled veggies exists due to personal effort.

I don't know any gardeners who want to patrol for insects and diseases. Well, that's not entirely true. I once knew an elderly woman in a retirement home who delighted in scouring her rose bushes for Japanese beetles, picking them off, and squishing them between her finger and thumb.

Generally, the rest of us want the tidiness of the EPCOT gardens at Disney World in Florida. We want the automated, mechanized gardens of the Jetsons. We want the luxury of picking our own food without the backbreaking nonsense of medieval farm labor.

Fortunately, today there's a system, a robot, and an app for that.

New Ways to Water

Back in the dark ages (roughly around the 1950s), innovations like sprinklers and drip hoses were considered a blessing. These were time-savers but still wasteful. Plus, you had to remember to turn them on. The next innovations were soaker hoses and automated timers. This next step forward was wonderful except that the system was still mindless. Who among us doesn't remember driving by a neighbor's property and seeing the automated sprinkler system running during a rain shower?

What was needed was a high-end approach. Farmers have been ahead of the game. They have been using satellites for years now to monitor crops in the field. Satellite images help the farmer spot if a particular area is getting too dry. Then, he or she can turn a watering system on or off, section by section as necessary. With the advent of smartphones, the farmer doesn't even have to be near the farm.

I know a commercial hemp farmer who has automated his entire watering, lighting, and fertilizing operation so that one person can grow and manage enough hemp sets to supply 100 acres.

So, where is the innovation for home gardeners?

Enter the smart sprinkler control system. In July 2019, the Wirecutter, a *New York Times* company, reviewed thirteen systems that will convert an outdated watering system to one that will supply water based on real-time weather and soil conditions, many in conjunction with a mobile app that monitors satellite, radar, and local weather station data.

All the smart watering systems tested by Wirecutter were under $250 and considered easy enough to install by the average homeowner. You still have to program a smart sprinkler system with the type of landscape it is expected to water, be it lawn, shrub border, or garden, but that is a minor "once and done" chore. The top systems will also allow for the addition of inline fertilizer injection, what one company cleverly calls "fertigation."

With one system, the gardener can eliminate water waste through overwatering, plant stress due to underwatering, and improper use of fertilizer (too much or too little).

Smart watering systems are great, but they still don't get us to a Jetsons lifestyle. For that, you need robots and drones.

Automated Laborers

So far, drones in the home garden are more playthings than laborers. Commercial farmers use them to spot problems in the field or to keep an eye on timberlands. Researchers in North Carolina are working on drones that will one day aid in crop pollination, a serious concern given the problems with bee populations.

Homeowners use drones to keep an eye on property borders. You can even use a drone to create a video diary of the progress of a garden or landscape. You may have heard that

Thomas Jefferson kept a detailed gardening journal for his estate at Monticello. As an inventor and innovator, I'm sure Jefferson would have been an early adopter of drones.

Homeowners are developing a taste for robots in the garden. The first "robot" in the landscape was the MowBot, introduced in 1969. It certainly didn't look like Rosie, the Jetsons' boxy housemaid. It was just a battery-operated mowing deck restricted by a wire that surrounded the area to be cut. Since then, MowBots have improved and other companies have gotten into the act, adding a solar-powered option in the 1990s.

According to the website Robots-and-Androids.com, today's robotic mowers can self-dock, analyze lawn growing conditions to determine when to roll out, alter mowing tracks to avoid creating wear patterns, and detect rainfall so they know when to stay inside.

Over in the garden, a similar robot (Tertill), developed by the inventor of Roomba, will patrol the garden plot. The owner's website, FranklinRobotics.com, notes the solar-powered gadget weed-whacks small, newly emerged weed seedlings before they become a large nuisance.

In another innovation, the website Gadget Reviews explains how you can make a small investment in one of several different static, solar-powered watering systems with motion detectors (see resources list). When the local bunny or the neighbor's cat shows up to violate your lettuce patch, one of these systems will shoot a harmless stream of water at the critter.

You can go whole hog and join the FarmBot revolution. FarmBot has to have been designed with technophiles in mind. It's billed as a "drag and drop" approach to gardening. Imagine if someone had taken the popular online game Farmville and brought it to life in your backyard.

According to the company's website, FarmBot isn't so much a single robot as a robotic system. It is available as a kit, or you can build your own from open-source instructions and materials. You construct a raised bed, then install a track frame that allows a programmable machine to carry out the instructions you send it electronically. In this case, having a mobile device or computer isn't just a novel option, it's a requirement.

Developers claim the entire package can be set up in about one hour. Once assembled, the robot will set seeds based on the design you create through its app and water the plants as they grow. Using its camera, it can detect unwanted plants and take them out using a small drill. The automated design can be a deterrent to unwanted guests too.

The system is designed to run on electricity but can be modified for solar power. It's pricey, but if you ever dreamed about gardening without getting your hands dirty, this might be what you are looking for.

Apt Apps

Of all the high-tech gardening options, garden apps are the ones with the most promise and, in my opinion, the most room to improve. As noted, all the newfangled gadgets for your landscape come with apps. Check any and every major plant or seed provider and you will find an online app to instruct you on how to grow just about anything, what to look out for, and what is recommended for your area.

Go to your favorite app store and type in "garden." Then, take a seat because you're going to be there awhile. Actually, the first thing you will need to do is sort the practical gardening apps from the online gardening games. For all the people who claim not to be interested in gardening, there sure are a lot of games based on building and maintaining a garden.

There are apps that will remind you when to water and fertilize every kind of plant in your landscape. There are apps to alert you to changing weather conditions so that you can plan your gardening activities accordingly.

The app I want is the one I frequently see on sci-fi programs. The intrepid hiker is lost in the woods. Oh, no! What can he eat to survive? He spies a plant, whips out his mobile device, scans the plant, and, just in time, discovers it is jimsonweed, and if he eats it, he will go stark raving mad—or die.

I have yet to find a plant app for homeowners that will reliably let you take a picture of a plant and identify it. Most are a version of twenty questions that gradually winnows down the probable answer to just a handful of possibilities. Some apps are doing a better job of identifying plant diseases. Most are still slow to load and leave the user with more questions than answers.

Looking Ahead

We have gone past EPCOT's promise of the "Garden of Tomorrow," based on sophisticated vertical and horizontal hydroponics.

In an ever-thirstier world, systems that can reduce the use of water in the garden without depleting our wallets will be well received. That could mean irrigation systems that monitor the individual plant, not just the garden plot.

Anything that reduces the use of pesticides would be a bonus. Several corporations are experimenting with the large-scale use of beneficial microbes that will help plants better access nutrients in the soil or increase their tolerance to environmental stress.

In a move that could be either wonderful or nightmarish, depending on your predilection, a European company, flora robotica, is experimenting with integrating robots and plants. According to its website, its goal is "to develop and investigate closely linked symbiotic relationships between robots and natural plants and to explore the potentials of a plant-robot society able to produce architectural artifacts and living spaces."

Is that a step too far? Maybe. I'm happy to have help with my gardening chores, but I'm not sure I'm ready to merge with my garden buddies yet.

Resources

Bellinger, Lawrence S. Self-propelled random motion lawnmower. Patent US3698523A, filed October 20, 1969, and issued October 17, 1972. https://patents.google.com/patent/US3698523.

"FarmBot Open Source CNC Farming." FarmBot. Accessed February 5, 2020. https://farm.bot/.

"Flora Robotica: Societies of Symbiotic Robot-Plant Bio-Hybrids as Social Architectural Artifacts." flora robotica. Accessed February 5, 2020. https://www.florarobotica.eu/.

"Lawn Mower Robots." Robots-and-Androids.com. Accessed February 5, 2020. http://www.robots-and-androids.com/lawn-mower-robots.html.

Mok, Kimberley. "Flora Robotica: Let the Robots Tend to Your Gardens." The New Stack. December 24, 2016. https://thenewstack.io/flora-robotica-let-robots-tend-gardens/.

Pattison Tuohy, Jennifer. "The Best Smart Sprinkler Controller." The Wirecutter. Last modified July 23, 2019. https://thewirecutter.com/reviews/best-smart-sprinkler-controller/.

Stinger. "Best Motion-Activated Sprinklers That Are Worth Buying in 2020." Gadget Reviews. Last modified February 14, 2020. https://gadgets-reviews.com/review/832-best-motion-activated-sprinklers.html#ixzz6Et6GOjNi.

Herb Crafts Using Recycled Materials

🐦 Autumn Damiana 🐦

A nyone who grows herbs or cooks with them will find at one time or another that they have more than they know what to do with. One of the easiest ways to use an overabundance from your garden and kitchen or to salvage that wilting flower bouquet is to make them into herb crafts. The projects I have outlined here do just that, and they are also very economical because they make use of common recyclable items you probably already have around the house.

I first began to experiment with "recycled art" when I worked with children, and the budget for crafts was so pitifully low that I had to turn to parents and ask them to contribute toilet paper rolls, milk cartons, and scrap paper so that we could conserve our money for things like glitter glue and paint. Thus, I discovered that it really is possible to make low-cost, fun, and functional crafts using recycled materials.

As with any craft you are trying for the first time, definitely read through all the directions first so that you get a feeling for what you will be making and there won't be any surprises later on. With that said, let's start crafting!

Easy Herb Sachet

This project can take only fifteen minutes if you opt for the no-sew version, but decorating and customizing it will take longer. You can use any t-shirt for this craft, but the longer the sleeves, the better. The fabric that is the most breathable and will have the best results is 100 percent cotton, but any cotton blend will work. This will make a large sachet that is wider than it is tall, but it will hold plenty of dried herbs.

Here is a short list of herbs, flowers, and spices to use (many of which are also natural insect repellents!): allspice, basil, bay, cardamom, cedar wood, chamomile, cinnamon, citrus peels, cloves, eucalyptus, gardenia, jasmine, lavender, lemon balm, lilac, mint, nutmeg, peppercorns, pine needles, rose, rosemary, star anise, and thyme.

Materials needed:
    Clean, old t-shirt
    Scissors
    Hot glue gun
    Small safety pin
    2 feet of thin ribbon

Dried herb blend

Essential oils (optional)

Embellishments: embroidery thread and needle, buttons, sequins, rhinestones, glitter glue, etc. (optional)

Lay out your t-shirt on a flat surface and smooth out the wrinkles. Pick which sleeve looks the nicest, as this will become your sachet. Cut off the sleeve as close to the shirt as possible in a line running parallel to the hem of the sleeve. (If you are using a long-sleeve t-shirt, pick any length from the hem you would like.) Put away the rest of the t-shirt to use for something else.

Turn the sleeve inside out and round off the corners where you have cut it. Line up the cut edges as close as possible, and glue these together with the hot glue gun (either high temp or low temp is fine). Allow the glue to cool and set for 5–10 minutes. Then, turn the sleeve right-side out.

Locate the seam that runs along the inside of the sleeve, where the armpit of the shirt was. Snip two vertical slits, one on either side of the seam in the top layer only of the hem. Next, take your safety pin and fasten it through one end of your ribbon. Push the safety pin through one of the vertical slits. Use the pin to thread the ribbon through the hem of the sleeve and out the other slit. Remove the pin, and now you have a drawstring on the side of the sachet.

You should use dried herbs as filler, since fresh ones can stain or become moldy. Break them up a bit (especially the whole spices) to release more of their scent. Add a few drops of essential oil if you like.

If you want to, you can also take your sachet to the next level with various embellishments. Some may prefer to sew up the bottom of the sachet on a sewing machine, but hand embroidery looks really nice too. Children may want to glue on buttons (bonus points if these are recycled from another garment!), sequins, and rhinestones. No matter what you apply, make sure your decorations are not too close to the hem on the sachet, or they could make it harder to cinch it closed. Use your sachets in dresser drawers or closets, as dream pillows, or as seasonal gifts.

Herb Candle Luminary

I keep seeing these papier-mâché lanterns online that people are creating using pressed and dried flowers and herbs, and while they are beautiful, they are a hassle to make and are very fragile. This project is a shortcut that not only looks the same but is also more durable and helps you skip a few steps. I love making this project after a birthday party or other holiday celebration, when I have an excess of tissue paper left over from gift-giving. There are several stages when you need to let the jar dry, but you can speed up this process by putting it on a foil-lined cookie sheet in the oven on the lowest setting.

Materials needed:
>   Empty wide-mouth glass jar (from pickles, jam/jelly, applesauce, pasta sauce, etc.)
>   Used tissue paper
>   Small foam paint brush
>   White glue
>   Pressed and dried herbs and flowers
>   Ribbon, 1 foot or more
>   Battery-powered candle or tea light
>   Hot glue gun (optional)

Wash the jar and remove all labels. Take your sheets of tissue paper and lay them out on a table. It doesn't matter how crumpled or torn they are—do your best to smooth each sheet flat. Then, tear the tissue paper into pieces, around 1–2 inches square. Do not cut the tissue paper! You want the pieces to blend together and form a layer, which doesn't work when you have too many hard edges.

Using your foam brush, add a coat of pure white glue all over the outside of your glass jar. Let that dry completely. This will help the tissue paper stick. Then, mix up some papier-mâché glue in a disposable dish or container (such as a paper cup). I start with half white glue and half water and adjust from there. You want your glue to be thin enough to paint it on with the foam brush, but not so thin that it runs.

Next, hold the jar by the threads at the top. Dip your brush into the glue mixture and add a thin coat to a small section. Stick some tissue pieces onto that section, and then use more glue mixture on your brush to mash those tissue pieces down, pasting them onto the jar. They will lie flat but have a lot of wrinkles in them, which is fine. Repeat this process all over the jar until you have built up two or three layers. You can do the bottom of the jar if you want, but you should *not* go over the rim at the top. Again, let this dry completely.

Now get your pressed and dried herbs and flowers. Leaves look really nice on this project, as do flowers like hydrangeas and violets, which have see-through petals. You can use a coating of pure white glue to stick them onto the jar. Then, repeat the above instructions to add one layer of tissue paper over them, mashing the tissue into place so that it is snug around the herbs and flowers—basically laminating them.

When everything is dry, glue a piece of ribbon around the jar threads with pure white glue, or a use a hot glue gun. If the ribbon is long enough, you can simply tie it around the jar. Now your luminary is ready to use. You can put battery-powered candles in the jar to illuminate it, but because there is a layer of glass between the candle and the papier-mâché, you can also use an actual candle, such as a tea light.

This project is simple to store, but if you decide you no longer need it, you can soak off the paper and herbs, throw those away, and then recycle the glass. If you want to make several luminaries at once, such as for a party, you can make them assembly-line style. It's also a big hit for a crafting afternoon with friends!

Plastic Bottle Bird Feeder

Anything we can all do collectively to keep plastic bottles out of the landfill by transforming them into something else is a win-win—for us because they are free and for the planet because it reduces plastic waste. This bird feeder does both. Of course, the best part is bird-watching when they come to feed and knowing that you will help sustain these birds in the winter months or whenever food is scarce.

The best ingredient in any birdseed is sunflower seeds, either whole or hulled. You can also add chopped nuts, especially peanuts, into your mix. Birds also like safflower seeds, cracked corn, white millet, and dried fruit, but they appreciate greens too. Try chopping up anise, basil, cilantro, dill, fennel, oregano, parsley, rosemary, or thyme and adding them to your bird feeder mix. Obviously, what birds like to eat really depends on what kind of birds you have! See the resources at the end of the article.

Materials needed:

Plastic bottle, no more than 32 ounces, with a wide cap
(Juice, sports drinks, and flavored water all have suitable bottles.)

Short and wide plastic tub, around 6 inches in diameter
(Use the kind that fresh salsa, guacamole, and hummus are packaged in or use a small plastic plant drip tray.)

Adhesive remover

2 wood disposable chopsticks

Coarse sandpaper

Industrial glue (I use E6000)

Craft knife

2 feet twine or long shoelace

Birdseed blend

The most important part of this craft is the process of preparing the materials. Remove the labels from the plastic, wash each piece thoroughly, and let them dry. Use an adhesive remover for the labels if you have to, but don't leave adhesive on anything! Birds can stick to this and it will harm the bird as it tries to become unstuck. It is also very important how you wash and dry the plastic. If there is any residue left inside the bottle or the tub, it can grow bacteria or make it hard to glue the plastic together. You should also wash the chopsticks, let them dry, and sand them down if they are not completely clean.

Next, rough up the top of the bottle's cap and the center of the inside of the plastic tub with the sandpaper—this will help the glue grab both pieces. Glue the top of the bottle cap to the inside of the plastic tub, as centered as possible. Let the glue dry or cure at least overnight, but leaving it for a day or two is preferable.

In the meantime, take the plastic bottle and with your craft knife, cut four triangular holes around it, equally spaced and as close as possible to the neck of the bottle. They should measure about ½ inch wide at the bottom (you can enlarge the holes later if necessary). *Use caution* with this step—the plastic is very thick near the top. Then, take one chopstick and cut it in half with the craft knife. You can do this by making shallow cuts in a circle around it and then snapping it in half.

Screw the bottle onto the cap. Glue the whole chopstick across the bottom of the plastic tub, lining it up with two of the holes. This will make two perches for the birds to eat out of the feeder. Take the broken chopstick and glue it perpendicular to the other, lining it up with the remaining two holes in the bottle.

Last, use your craft knife to cut two small holes opposite each other on the sides of the bottle, near the bottom. Again, *be careful* when cutting—the plastic near the bottom is also strong. Thread one end of the twine or shoelace through one of the holes, and the other end through the other hole, until both ends hang out the top of the bottle. Knot these together tightly a few times, pull the twine or shoelace up from the bottom, and you have a loop to hang on a hook or a branch.

To fill your feeder, simply turn the configuration upside-down, unscrew the tub/cap, and then fill the bottle. Replace the tub/cap, invert the bottle, and the seed will spill out into the tub, which the birds can eat from. You can hang the feeder outside on a porch or patio, in the branches of a tree, or anywhere else that you can see the feeder and that gives the birds a sheltered spot to eat.

Garden Journal Accordion Book

Here is a really enjoyable and educational project to do with children. It involves arts and crafts, learning about herbs and flowers, and of course recycling. You can make it as simple or as complex as you like depending on the ages of the children you are working with.

A "garden journal" can be whatever you want it to be. You can keep basic records from year to year of what you plant and your observations. You can also use it simply as a pictorial guide for plant identification. If you don't have a garden, the book can be about plants collected on walks or hikes, brought home from trips, or even herbs used in your kitchen—with accompanying recipes!

Materials needed:

Standard paper grocery bag

Scissors

Pencil

Glue

8 used 3 × 5-inch index cards (Left over from school assignments, lists, notes, old recipes, etc. Only use if they are blank on one side.)

Ruler

2 pieces of cardboard or card stock measuring approximately 6 × 8 inches

2–3 feet ribbon or string (optional)

First, you need to prepare your bag. There are many folds all over paper grocery bags, and you will be working with these. To start, pull off the handles and discard them. Then, open the bag and set it upright on the floor. Starting at a corner of the bag, cut all the way down the edge to the bottom. Turn the bag over and cut out the rectangle that makes up the bottom of the bag and discard this as well. You should now have one long piece of paper with the side folds still intact.

Now it gets a little trickier. There is a slight crease that runs parallel to the lower edge of the bag—you can see on the sides of the bag toward the bottom there are V-shaped folds that help the bag collapse flat, and the crease runs just above the point on each V. Trace along this crease with your pencil and then cut straight along the line, removing the lower portion of the bag.

Each of the two "panels" of the folded side pieces are the perfect width to glue on a 3 × 5-inch index card, so you need to accordion-fold the entire bag close to the size of these panels. To do this, use your ruler to divide each of the two large 12 inch front and back panels of the bag into even thirds, marking the lines at 4 and 8 inches. These thirds will be a bit bigger than the side panels.

The last step is to make your book. Ignore which direction the existing folds go, and accordion-fold (like a paper fan) the whole thing using those folds and the four lines you drew on the larger panels as your guide. If you have done this correctly, you should have 10 "pages" in your book that you can trim to be ½ inch or so taller than the index cards. The book pages will be somewhat uneven, since not all of the 10 panels are the same size, but the front and back cover will hide this.

To add the covers, simply use two panels of cardboard or card stock that are cut slightly larger than the book. Recycled boxes from cereal, crackers, granola bars, and so on are perfect for this, but I like to use pretty greeting cards that I save. Glue one cover to the front page and one to the back page of your book. If you want to get really fancy, center a piece of ribbon or string on the back page of your book before gluing the back cover on. When dry, this can tie your book shut.

Use the index cards to put pictures of your herb, flower, or leaf along with name, variety or species, and any other notes, and then glue them to the pages of your book. Older children may want to sketch or draw the plants, while younger children can trace and color them in or make hammered botanical prints.

To make hammered prints, place an index card on a cutting board and arrange your plant on it the way you would like it to look. Lay a paper towel carefully over both, and then *gently* tap the plant all over many times with a hammer or palm-sized river rock (little ones will need extra help with this part). When the image of the plant starts to bleed through into the paper towel, remove it, peel off the plant matter, and you will have your print. It will take practice to get this technique just right, but when you do, you will love the results. Some plants work better than others, but that's part of the discovery process.

One of the most remarkable things about this project is that when it is finished, you can open and extend the accordion book, which will stand up on a table, and therefore display all the pages at once. This makes it a great choice for school projects like book reports, science fairs, or even art exhibitions.

Making projects with recycled materials can become addictive. Over time, you will start looking at the common "throwaway" or single-use items you have in your home in a totally new way. Why not combine that vision with your love of herb crafts, as I have? With a little inspiration and the endless possibilities that the internet provides, I'll bet that you can come up with some totally new projects on your own. Not only will you be a happy crafter, but the planet will thank you for recycling and keeping yet more waste out of a landfill.

Recommended Resources

Here is some helpful information to make your own flower and herb press: https://blog.mountainroseherbs.com/plant-press

Find information about the types of birds that live in your area: https://en.wikipedia.org/wiki/Lists_of_birds_by_region

General information about drying herbs for food or crafts: https://www.thespruce.com/how-to-dry-and-store-herbs-1403397

A great resource for how to press and dry flowers and herbs: http://www.preservedgardens.com/how-to-press.htm

More information about pressing flowers, including how to iron them: https://www.proflowers.com/blog/how-to-press-flowers

A how-to for pressing flowers and herbs, using many different techniques: https://www.bhg.com/gardening/design/projects/make-pressed-flowers/

Grow a Living Wall

~ Kathy Vilim ~

Ready to grow *up*? Vertical gardening has increased in popularity in recent years. Although the idea of growing living walls is not new (the Hanging Gardens of Babylon, which date back to 600 BCE, come to mind), it has caught on as a unique way to add greenery to your backyard, patio, or balcony. You can dress up an old fence or bring a green wall into your home or office. When entertaining, you will find that living walls are conversation starters. They are focal points that create immediate visual interest.

When it comes to growing vertically, there are so many options. How do you decide what kind of wall to make? The plants you choose will

give you different looks. Succulents, herbs, vegetables, ferns, bromeliads, moss—almost any plant can live vertically, even tropical houseplants. Living walls can provide a place to grow plants in otherwise unfavorable conditions, such as yards with rocky soil.

Planning a Vertical Garden

First, what is your goal? What is the purpose for your living wall? Do you want a privacy wall between your yard and your neighbors? Perhaps a wall using aromatic herbs and vines would suit your purpose. Are you tight on space but want a vegetable garden? Free-standing wall systems can turn your balcony into a food-producing garden. Do you want to bring culinary herbs closer to your kitchen? Create a living wall of herbs outside the kitchen door. Do you live in a northern climate and don't want to leave a living wall outside in winter? Herbs can be grown indoors, creating a living wall right in your sunny kitchen. Or perhaps you want to attract pollinators with blooms. If so, create a wall of flowering plants near your favorite garden chair. From there you could enjoy watching the winged visitors you will be attracting to your garden.

A living wall can also take the form of living art, framed and hung on a wall, letting the plants create a picture, if you will. I am much impressed by the wall designs that utilize a picture frame. These can be placed indoors, adding greenery to an office, or hung on a wall, bringing a finished indoor look to an outdoor room.

Location

Your living wall will be a success if you first consider the lighting conditions of the space you have in mind. Lots of sun is needed for growing vegetables or succulents. Flowering plants will dry out more quickly when planted vertically, so you will want to give them partial shade. Of course, if you are creating a fern garden, light shade is also essential.

Wall System Options

Once you've determined the goal for your vertical wall garden, you can look at the different wall frame system options available to you. Consider the following: How much space do you have for your living wall? A large living wall will be much heavier than a smaller one, and you will need to be sure it is hung with sturdy brackets. Are you handy with tools? Do you want to build your own vertical garden from scratch? Or are you more comfortable using a premade wall hanging system and focusing instead on designing and maintaining the plants? There are a number of interesting living wall frames and pockets out there these days, and judging by the variety of wall systems, it appears that vertical gardening is seeing an increase in popularity.

Go Eco-Friendly

A living wall garden can also be created by repurposing found objects, allowing room for creativity and even whimsy. One of the more unusual ideas I have seen was a living wall made of repurposed ammunition boxes which were turned into herb boxes, made by designer and gardener Ryan Benoit. The boxes were then hung by chains in front of a wall.

Maintenance

One thing you will want to consider is watering and fertilizing. Plants require maintenance in order to thrive, and vertical gardens are no different. You can buy a wall system that comes complete with drip irrigation, or you can add a drip irrigation system to the vertical wall you create. You might prefer to hand water with a wand. A living wall can even be grown hydroponically, according to gardening author Shawna Coronado, who recommends hydroponic systems for thirsty pollinator blooming plants.

As far as fertilizing, I prefer using a liquid fertilizer for the vertical garden. I use Haven Brand's natural brew tea (a.k.a. "moo poo tea") made from manure and sold in convenient tea bags. Fish emulsion also works well.

How to Make a Vertical Italian Herb Pallet Garden

My neighbor Judith asked me to make her a vertical wall garden for her herbs. Judith is Italian and loves to cook Tuscan cuisine, so it was a no-brainer that she'd like to grow culinary herbs for Italian dishes in her vertical garden. For this project, I chose to use an eco-friendly repurposed wooden pallet. We are going to take a 40 × 48-inch pallet and cut it down in size to make two pallets. We painted one yellow and one blue, and they hang together next to her kitchen door, within easy reach.

There are many benefits to choosing a pallet for your vertical garden. Pallets take little space, making them perfect for the walls of patios or balconies. They can be hung on a wall or used standing with landscape blocks. A culinary herb pallet garden like Judith's can be hung beside the kitchen door, putting herbs within easy reach.

One advantage of using pallets is that they are easy to find, sometimes abandoned behind markets. Plus, often you can pick them up for free! Check out 1001pallets.com for ideas.

When choosing a pallet, get one that is marked "HT," which means the wood has been heat treated in a kiln rather than treated with chemicals. Reusing a pallet is environmentally responsible, as you are keeping wood out of a landfill. But if you prefer, you can also purchase brand new pallets.

You can choose to use the pallet raw, stained, or painted. If you choose to stain or paint, I recommend sanding first. Judith likes color, so we chose to paint her first pallet sky blue and the second pallet yellow. The two pallets were going to be placed next to each other on the wall outside her kitchen door. In order to do this, I had to saw the big pallet into two halves.

Supplies needed:
> Saw
>
> 40 × 48-inch pallet
>
> Sandpaper
>
> Paint or stain (optional)
>
> Landscape fabric
>
> Staple gun
>
> Staples
>
> Drill
>
> Lightweight potting soil with perlite and/or worm castings
>
> Liquid fertilizer

Suggested Italian herbs:
> Arugula
>
> Bay leaves

Chervil

Chives

Cilantro/coriander

Curled parsley

Italian parsley

Marjoram

Oregano

Paprika

Rosemary

Saffron

Sage

Sweet basil

Thyme

Saw the pallet in half perpendicular to the boards. Lay pallets flat on the ground and sand. If desired, paint or stain pallets. Place landscape fabric across the back of the pallets, wrap the fabric around the sides, and staple it securely so soil doesn't escape.

Make pockets for the front of the pallets using landscape fabric and stapling, letting the fabric hang in the space between the wood strips.

Drill holes and screw the pallets directly into the wall. Small pallets should not require an additional bracket.

Fill pockets with soil halfway. Then fill in with plants, making sure to place them close together. This will result in a full look when they grow in.

Be sure to place trailing herbs, such as rosemary (*Rosmarinus officinalis* 'Prostratus'), in the front. 'Huntington Carpet' is a good variety for trailing rosemary used in cooking. Fertilize and enjoy your wall.

This pallet garden is also a welcoming sign to any visitors entering the house through the kitchen door. In her backyard Judith also maintains a raised bed vegetable garden of spinach, tomatoes, garlic, zucchini, and eggplant. If you have always wanted to have a culinary herb garden close at hand, you have just found a great solution using vertical pallets.

If you want to use a whole pallet and stand it on the ground, create a base with landscape blocks.

Creating a Vertical Garden Using Pockets

Today, there are many different wall systems available for the vertical gardener to choose from. One of the most interesting is the pocket wall system. Pockets made of felt are mounted next to each other until you have a vertical wall that will accommodate as many plants as your space requires. Pocket walls are a wonderful way to dress up an old fence, or you can create a colorful blooming wall that will attract pollinators.

A nice feature of the pockets is flexibility. You can add as many pockets as you want, increasing the size of your garden over time. The pockets also make it easy to change plants. If you want to remove a plant, you can do so without upsetting the rest of the garden.

Wall pockets can handle many types of plants, including vegetables, herbs, tropical plants, flowering plants, and even ferns. It is best to use plants that hang down a bit, so that when they grow in, they will cover the pocket's fabric.

Suggested Plants for Attracting Pollinators

If you are planting a vertical wall garden to attract pollinators, you will want to select plants that provide nourishing nectar to native bees, hummingbirds, butterflies, and moths. Why not use native plants? There are native varieties of the herb sage (*Salvia*), for example, in every region of the United States. Look for plants without deep roots that can live in containers.

In general, hummingbirds prefer red tubular blossoms. Butterflies, on the other hand, prefer open blossoms that they can perch on to drink nectar.

To find native plants that attract pollinators in your area, visit these websites:

The Hummingbird Society: hummingbirdsociety.org/humming
    bird-flowers
Xerces Society: xerces.org/pollinator-conservation/plant-lists
US Dept of Agriculture Natural Resource Conservation Service:
    plants.sc.egov.usda.gov/java
Lady Bird Johnson Wildflower Center: wildflower.org/plants
    -main

Construction

Wall pockets are super easy to install. The pocket system I like best is called Wally Pro Pockets by manufacturer Wally-Gro. These are lightweight felt containers measuring 24 × 15 inches. Besides single pockets, WallyGro carries 3-across and

5-across pockets. Each pocket comes with drywall anchors and screws for hanging on any type of surface.

To hang the pockets on a wall or fence, first draw a line to indicate where each pocket will go. The pockets are going to be hung next to each other horizontally. Start with the first row near the top of your wall or fence and drill holes, two per pocket. Slide the manufacturer's fasteners into the holes and attach the pockets. Allow them to overlap a bit. Then create the next rows below.

Planting

Fill the pockets halfway with soil. If installing drip irrigation, the manufacturer instructs to install it at this point behind the tongue of the pocket. Place hanging plants toward the front of the pocket and taller plants in back.

Hand Watering

Wally Pro Pockets have a felt exterior and are lined with a waterproof barrier made from eco-friendly recycled bottles. This keeps water from getting to your wall. Note that the lining only extends 25 percent of the way up the front panel; this is to give the soil a chance to breathe. It is recommended that, if you are hand watering, the soil should be packed at a 2-inch slant, lower at the back, thus creating a reservoir for watering. This will prevent water from saturating the front of the pocket. When watering, aim toward the back panel of the pocket. Give each pocket approximately 2 cups of water. Drip kits are also available.

Voilà! You have just created a new focal point for your outdoor room or garden. Visitors will enjoy sitting outside and looking at this colorful blooming wall. If you've used pollinator-friendly plants, butterflies and hummingbirds will also visit. There is nothing like watching the antics of a hummingbird or following the graceful flight of a butterfly while sipping afternoon tea. Why not dress up a fence and provide food for pollinators at the same time?

Living Walls Are Popping Up All Over the Place

In urban settings, living wall gardens are popping up more and more these days. All over the world, landscape architects and builders are increasingly focusing their attention on adding green walls and green roofs to tall buildings. They have been creating vertical parks in commercial spaces that offer visitors a chance to drink in nature while they walk between buildings or sit on restful garden benches in outdoor courtyards. Besides creating clean air for us, these living walls can also offer food for pollinators if flowering plants are used.

Living walls have a therapeutic healing effect both indoors and outdoors. Adding a living wall to a room instantly adds a feeling of calm and relaxation. This is where the art frame type of wall system works nicely. Art frame kits include a box divided up with cells for planting, a frame, and a drip kit. The framed kits let you "paint a picture" with your plants. If you are using succulents, you will want to purchase smaller cells for a tighter look.

As the world moves forward to a greener future, it appears that living wall gardens will be a solution to many contemporary problems: gardening in a small space or on a balcony, bringing herbs closer to the kitchen, repurposing materials, welcoming visitors to a back patio that attracts pollinators, and bringing nature's therapeutic benefits closer to people living in urban spaces.

Vertical gardening is a great trend for all of us—and for the planet.

Resources

Benoit, Ryan. "Ammo Can Herb Garden." Ryan Benoit Design. Accessed February 6, 2020. https://ryanbenoitdesign.com/ammo-can-vertical-herb-garden/.

Coronado, Shawna. *Grow a Living Wall*. Minneapolis, MN: Cool Springs Press, 2015.

Dunnett, Nigel, and Noel Kingsbury. *Planting Green Roofs and Living Walls*. Portland, OR: Timber Press, 2008.

Fell, Derek. *Vertical Gardening: Grow Up, Not Out, for More Vegetables and Flowers in Much Less Space*. New York: Rodale Books, 2011.

Plant
Profiles

Plant Profiles

This section features spotlights on individual herbs, high-lighting their cultivation, history, and culinary, crafting, and medicinal uses. Refer to the key below for each plant's sun and water needs, listed in a helpful at-a-glance table.

Key to Plant Needs	
Sun	
Shade	—
Partial shade	☀
Partial sun	☀ ☀
Full sun	☀ ☀ ☀
Water	
Water sparingly	💧
	💧 💧
Water frequently	💧 💧 💧

USDA Hardiness Zones

The United States is organized into zones according to the average lowest annual winter temperature, indicating a threshold for cold tolerance in the area. This USDA Plant Hardiness Zone Map uses the latest available data. For best results, plant herbs that can withstand the climate of their hardiness zone(s) and bring less hardy plants indoors during colder weather. Seek additional resources for high summer temperatures, as these can vary within zones.

It is helpful to keep track of temperatures and frost dates in your neighborhood or check with a local gardening center or university extension for the most up-to-date record. Climate change and local topography will also affect your growing space, so compensate accordingly.

USDA Plant Hardiness Zone Map

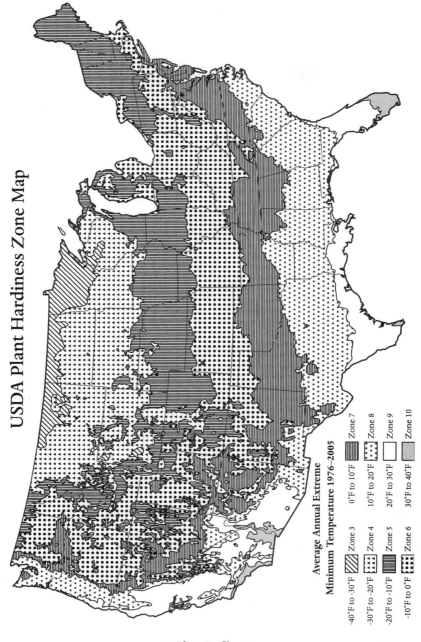

**Average Annual Extreme
Minimum Temperature 1976–2005**

-40°F to -30°F	Zone 3	0°F to 10°F	Zone 7
-30°F to -20°F	Zone 4	10°F to 20°F	Zone 8
-20°F to -10°F	Zone 5	20°F to 30°F	Zone 9
-10°F to 0°F	Zone 6	30°F to 40°F	Zone 10

USDA Plant Hardiness Zone Map (Cont.)

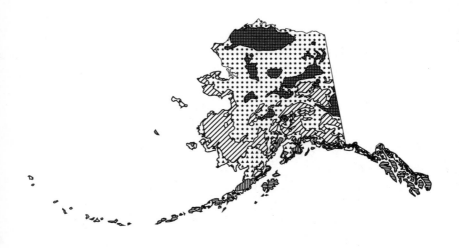

Average Annual Extreme
Minimum Temperature 1976–2005

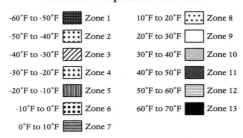

-60°F to -50°F	Zone 1	10°F to 20°F	Zone 8
-50°F to -40°F	Zone 2	20°F to 30°F	Zone 9
-40°F to -30°F	Zone 3	30°F to 40°F	Zone 10
-30°F to -20°F	Zone 4	40°F to 50°F	Zone 11
-20°F to -10°F	Zone 5	50°F to 60°F	Zone 12
-10°F to 0°F	Zone 6	60°F to 70°F	Zone 13
0°F to 10°F	Zone 7		

Ginger

≫ Anne Sala ≪

Knobby, brown, and a bit dirty-looking, ginger appears out of place in the produce aisle of the local grocery store. Surrounded by vibrant greens, reds, and yellows, this spice shows no outward sign of all the dazzling flavor and medicinal healing powers held within.

More than 5,000 years ago, the inhabitants of tropical Southeast Asia introduced their trading partners to the rhizome *Zingiber officinale*, a magical spice that cured nearly every ailment. Its spicy, fruity flavor and aroma were unlike any other known. It was quickly incorporated into the medicine bags of neighboring China and India. From there, its popularity spread to the Middle East, Africa, ancient Rome, and

Ginger	
Species	*Zingiber officinale*
Zone	7–10
Needs	☀☀ 💧💧
Soil pH	5.5–6.5
Size	3–4 ft. tall

medieval Europe. Later, the easily transported "knobs" were brought to the Americas, Caribbean, and Australia. Today, ginger is a lucrative crop in several of these countries, and it has left its mark on many nations' favorite recipes.

Ginger is a member of the Zingiberaceae family along with turmeric, galangal, and cardamom. The family also includes ornamental gingers and "bitter" ginger, neither of which is edible. The fibrous rhizome is a perennial, and every year, it produces grass-like shoots from nodes that can grow up to three feet tall. This shoot unfurls yet more grass, or lance-like leaves that radiate outward. Yellow and purple flowers bloom on their own separate shoots that also rise up from the ginger root.

To flourish, ginger needs warm, tropical temperatures, dappled shade, and moist—but not soggy—soil. The ginger used in cooking is thought to not grow in the wild naturally, which makes sense to me since humans have been cultivating it for so long. That would also explain why the plant's shoots are susceptible to wind damage.

Growing Ginger at Home

It is possible to grow ginger in more temperate regions in a pot that can be brought inside when temperatures cool or as an indoor plant in a sunny location. I grew ginger in a sunny window of my Minnesota home. I gave it a splash of water every afternoon, and it rewarded me with shoots that grew noticeably taller each day. The rhizome itself had very thin tan and pink skin. I haven't tasted it yet because it's still too young.

To grow your own, you may buy a ginger plant that's already sprouted, or try your luck growing some from ginger purchased at the supermarket. If you decide on the latter, look for organic ginger that is not withered or dried out and that has little pyramid-like nodes pushing through the skin.

If your "hand" of ginger is large, you may break off a piece with nodes on it. Leave the piece out on your counter for at least twenty-four hours to allow the cut part to dry out. When ready to plant, place potting soil in a wide, shallow pot with drainage holes. Create an indentation in the soil so the ginger lies about one inch below the surface, and plant it node-side up. Cover with soil and gently tamp it down.

Water well the first time, then keep the soil moist, but not soggy, thereafter. If the soil is too wet, the ginger will rot. After a couple of weeks, your patience will be rewarded with a green shoot poking through the soil.

When harvesting your ginger, don't toss the leaves in the compost—they're edible! Mince a few leaves and sprinkle them on top of a dish as you would chives or parsley.

You can harvest the ginger after six months, if you want (simply cut off the shoots, wash, and prepare for your meal), or you can replant it and let it grow until the ginger is big enough to break off a piece to use. Then rebury the main part of the rhizome so it can continue to grow. You may find you never buy ginger in the store again!

Healing with Ginger

"Let food be thy medicine, and let medicine be thy food." This famous quote is attributed to Hippocrates around 400 BCE.

Perhaps he was thinking about ginger when he said that. This sentiment is also fundamental in both Ayurvedic and Chinese medicine, which were in use for centuries before Hippocrates's time. In those ancient sciences, ginger is considered one of the most important spices for its ability to act as a warming agent in the body. It was used to increase circulation, relieve pain, reduce nausea, and ease cold symptoms.

When Western-style medicine turned its attention to ginger, studies confirmed the age-old wisdom of the East: ginger was not a placebo. It contains antioxidants that are effective at reducing inflammation that damages joints. Studies also confirmed its effectiveness as an antiseptic, to manage diabetes, and to ease symptoms of heart disease. Furthermore, its ability to quell nausea rivaled the effectiveness of antinausea drugs prescribed to chemotherapy patients, but without the side effects. It is also safe to give to pregnant and nursing women (under the guidance of their health care provider).

Homemade Dried Ginger Poultice

This recipe serves two purposes. The first is to prove how simple it is to make your own ginger powder, which will come in handy if you start growing your own ginger and need more uses for it. The second is to demonstrate how easy it is to use ginger medicinally. According to Ramya Venkateshwaran of *Wild Turmeric*, ginger poultices are an age-old remedy for joint pain and sinus headaches in India.

Please be aware that ginger placed directly on the skin can cause a burning sensation that may last for several minutes. Please gauge your body's reaction by applying a test patch first. In my instructions, I place the poultice in a piece of cloth, but you are welcome to apply directly to your skin. Just be sure to not get it in your eyes if using it on your forehead. I would not recommend using it on other parts of your face.

For the dried ginger:

    1 "hand" of never-frozen ginger

    Sharp knife

    Cutting board

    Food dehydrator or oven

    Baking sheet

    Electric spice grinder

    Fine mesh sieve

    Large bowl

    Funnel

    1 or more glass jars with airtight lids

Break or cut off the ginger's "fingers" and wash all the pieces carefully to remove any hidden dirt. Dry thoroughly with paper towels. Peeling the ginger is optional.

Cut the pieces into small chunks with the sharp knife on the cutting board. You want the pieces to be small so they dry easily, but not so small that the rhizome releases its liquid.

Either scrape the ginger into the food dehydrator, according to its instructions, or spread it on a baking sheet and bake on the oven's lowest setting. This could take 6–8 hours. Check the ginger occasionally. It is dry enough when the pieces no longer yield to pressure (think to yourself, if I accidentally stepped on this with bare feet, would it hurt?).

Transfer the pieces to the spice grinder and pulverize. Depending on how much you started with, you may want to process the ginger in batches.

Pour the ginger into the sieve placed over the bowl. Gently shake or stir the ginger so the powder falls through. If there are pieces of ginger left in the sieve, return them to the grinder to process again.

When all the ginger is sufficiently processed, use the funnel to help pour the powder into one or more storage jars. Seal tightly and store in a cool, dark location.

For the poultice:

Small bowl

2–3 tablespoons ginger powder

1–2 tablespoons boiling water

1 piece thin cloth, such as muslin or cheesecloth

Spoon

6 inches twine

In a small bowl, mix the ginger with the boiling water. Start with just a little water and mix. You are trying to create a thick but pliable paste.

Moisten the cloth with hot water and wring it out.

Spoon the ginger paste into the center of the cloth and fold up the sides to make a rectangular pack, or gather up the sides to create a ball of paste and tie it with twine.

Apply the ginger poultice to painful joints or the forehead for about 20 minutes. You may administer new poultices up to 3 times a day, as long as your skin shows no lasting signs of redness or irritation.

Cooking with Ginger

Now with a nod to Hippocrates, let's turn our attention to the food aspect of ginger. Below are two recipes that share two main ingredients that are treated differently. The first is a fairly quick "school night" meal, and the other has multiple steps that can be spread across several days if necessary.

Sheet Pan Glazed Ginger Chicken and Rice

Rachael Ray, a quick-meal expert, was the inspiration for this recipe. It is easy to double, but you may need to use two pans.

   1 tablespoon olive oil, plus more for oiling pan

   1 medium onion, diced

   1 3-inch piece of ginger, peeled and finely chopped

   1 tablespoon soy sauce

   2 teaspoons sesame oil

   8 boneless chicken thighs, with or without skin

   1 cup short-grain brown or white rice

   2½ cups water

   Salt to taste

   2 cups green beans, stems removed

   4 carrots, peeled and cut into matchsticks

   ¼ cup apricot preserves

   ⅓ cup hoisin sauce

   ⅛ cup orange juice

Preheat oven to 425°F. Lightly oil a large rimmed sheet pan.

Combine the onion, ginger, soy sauce, and sesame oil in a large bowl. Toss the chicken in the bowl until coated. Set aside.

Spread the rice onto the prepared pan and place the pan in the oven. Carefully pour the water into the pan and sprinkle with salt. Bake for 10–12 minutes.

Toss the carrots, oil, and a sprinkling of salt in a medium bowl.

Carefully open the oven and extend the rack with the pan on it. Gently stir the rice, then spread it into an even layer. Remove chicken from the marinade and settle on top of the rice. Reserve the marinade. Next, remove the carrots from the oil and nestle them between the chicken pieces. Reserve the oil. Return the pan to the oven and bake for 15 minutes.

Toss the green beans in the bowl with the reserved oil from the carrots, and mix the preserves, hoisin, and orange juice into the bowl with the reserved marinade.

Brush the chicken with the marinade mixture and then find places for the green beans. It is okay if they overlap the carrots and chicken. If there is any remaining marinade mixture, you can brush it on the carrots and green beans. Bake for 15 minutes or until the glaze is bubbly, the rice has absorbed the water, and the chicken's internal temperature reaches 165°F.

Serve immediately. Serves 4.

Baked Rice and Short Ribs

I love this recipe because it shows how ginger traveled in the pockets of traders all the way from Asia, through India, and into Africa. This style of rice is popular in India, where it is called *pilau*, as well as the east coast of Africa. In Somalia it is known as *bariis iskukaris*. On festive occasions, meat is added.

Since the recipe calls for short ribs, a notoriously tough cut of meat, I would suggest making this recipe on the weekend, when it won't matter if it takes a long time for the meat to fall apart. In fact, you can prepare the meat in advance. Another note: I use ancho chili powder in my house because my children refuse to eat anything spicy. Feel free to substitute something fresh or hotter if you prefer, such as a fresno chili or jalapeño.

For the ribs:

- 2–2½ tablespoons extra-virgin olive oil
- 2½ pounds boneless beef short ribs, cut into ½-inch pieces
- Salt
- 1 medium onion, chopped
- 4 garlic cloves, chopped
- 1 3-inch piece ginger, peeled, finely chopped
- 1 tablespoon tomato paste
- 1 tablespoon ancho chili powder
- 1 teaspoon ground cinnamon
- 1 teaspoon ground cumin
- 1 teaspoon ground coriander
- 1½ cups water

Heat 2 tablespoons oil in a large, heavy pot over medium heat. Working in batches, brown the meat and season with salt. Remove each batch while there are still pink spots, and transfer to a plate.

Once all the meat is cooked, add the additional oil to the pot if it looks dry, and toss in the onion, garlic, ginger, and tomato paste. After 1 minute, add the chili powder, cinnamon, cumin, and coriander. Continue stirring so the mixture does not burn, for about 6 minutes. Deglaze the pot with 1½ cups of water, scraping the pan to release the tasty browned bits.

Return the beef and juices to the pot. Bring to a simmer, cover, and cook on medium-low to low until beef starts to fall apart. This could be anywhere from 1½ hours to 3 hours. Add water occasionally if the meat is still tough but in danger of scorching. When the meat finally begins to fall apart, continue to cook uncovered until the liquid is almost gone. This should take an additional 20–30 minutes. Let cool, then coarsely shred meat. At this point, you may store the meat in the refrigerator for up to 3 days before finishing the dish.

For the rice:

    1 tablespoon unsalted butter, plus 1 tablespoon

    2 cups basmati rice

    Kosher salt

    2 teaspoons sugar

    2 tablespoons apple cider vinegar

    Salt to taste

    4 medium carrots, shredded (about 3 cups)

    ¼ cup golden raisins or dried currants

    ¼ teaspoon saffron threads, crushed

    6 peeled bananas for serving

    Harissa paste for serving

Preheat oven to 375°F. Butter a baking dish and sheet of foil and set aside.

Place the rice in a colander or large bowl and rinse it until the water loses its milky appearance. Pour the rice into a saucepan with enough fresh water to cover by 1 inch. Season generously with salt and bring to a boil. Simmer the rice until almost fully cooked, about 6–8 minutes. Quickly drain the rice in a colander and rinse with cold water, then drain thoroughly. Return the rice to the pan and set aside.

Store ginger in a resealable plastic bag in the freezer to keep it fresh longer. Take it out while you gather the rest of your ingredients, and it will be thawed enough to cut by the time you're ready to prepare it.

Stir together the sugar, vinegar, a big pinch of salt, and 1 tablespoon butter in a saucepan with ⅓ cup water. When it begins to simmer, add the carrots, raisins, and saffron, and return the mixture to a boil. Lower the heat and stir often until the water is mostly evaporated and the pan starts to sizzle. Mix this into the rice and add more salt if needed.

Spoon half the rice mixture into the prepared baking dish and smooth it into an even layer. Spread all the meat on top of the rice and then cover with the remaining rice. Seal the dish with the foil, butter side down, and bake for 45 minutes. Remove foil and bake for an additional 15 minutes.

Serve warm, with a peeled banana on the side. Mix in a little harissa (or another favorite hot sauce) for a burst of tangy heat. Serves 6.

Resources

"How to Use Ginger for Sinus Headaches: Ginger Poultice/Sukku Pathu." *Wild Turmeric* (blog), January 31, 2013. https://www.wildturmeric.net/dry-ginger-pastesukku-pathu-for-headache/.

Gladstar, Rosemary. *Rosemary Gladstar's Medicinal Herbs: A Beginner's Guide.* North Adams, MA: Storey Publishing, 2012.

PenzeyMoog, Caitlin. *On Spice: Advice, Wisdom, and History with a Grain of Saltiness.* New York: Skyhorse Publishing, 2019.

Simonds, Nina. *A Spoonful of Ginger: Irresistible, Health-Giving Recipes from Asian Kitchens*. New York: Alfred A. Knopf, 1999.

Suttie, Emma. "Ginger Is Medicine." Chinese Medicine Living. March 5, 2014. https://www.chinesemedicineliving.com/chinese-medicine/ginger-is-medicine/.

Thongtham, Normita. "Ginger Up." *Bangkok Post*, November 27, 2016. https://www.bangkokpost.com/life/social-and-life style/1145569/ginger-up.

Young, Jacqueline. *The Healing Path: The Practical Guide to the Holistic Traditions of China, India, Tibet, and Japan*. London: Thorsons, 2001.

Rhubarb

⇾ Sandra Kynes ⇽

A favorite during Victorian times, rhubarb was *de rigueur* in any respectable herb and vegetable garden well into the twentieth century. Rhubarb's popularity faded for a while, but after winning hearts and taste buds once again, this garden classic has made a stunning comeback. And it has returned with a much wider culinary repertoire beyond the quintessential rhubarb and strawberry pie. It is also gaining status as an ornamental plant, adding a dramatic flair to home and public gardens.

Also known as pie plant, rhubarb is a large herbaceous perennial with statuesque spikes of flowers and leaf stalks that look like oversize red celery. Winter hardy and resistant to drought,

Rhubarb	
Species	*Rheum rhabarbarum*
Zone	3–7
Needs	☀☀☀ 💧💧💧
Soil pH	5.5–6.5
Size	2–5 ft. tall & wide

a mature plant can spread about five feet across with stalks supporting a canopy of huge showy leaves that can be more than a foot wide. For me, rhubarb's distinctive earthy smell brings back childhood memories of playing hide-and-seek among the plants in my grandmother's garden.

Color does not indicate ripeness, and rhubarb stalks can range from light to bright pink to red and pale green. The stalks are at their best when at least ten to twelve inches long. Rhubarb's astringency is responsible for its unusual flavor, which is so tart that it is almost never eaten raw. While the roots have been used for medicinal purposes throughout the centuries, the leaves are poisonous and should never be consumed. Technically a vegetable, a court ruling in New York during the late 1940s proclaimed rhubarb a fruit because it was most often eaten as dessert.

Healing History of Rhubarb

Garden rhubarb has an exotic history and is believed to be a hybrid of Chinese rhubarb (R. *palmatum*), which is native to northwestern China and parts of Siberia. The roots and rhizomes of Chinese rhubarb have been used medicinally for thousands of years. The earliest description of it appeared in the herbal text *Shen Nung Pen Tsao Ching*, which is generally regarded as having been written in the second century CE. As an important trade commodity transported by camel caravan on the Silk Road, rhubarb made its way into India and Persia and eventually to Europe. It was known to the ancient Greeks and Romans, who used the root for a range of ailments. Known as *da huang*, rhubarb is still an important herb in Traditional Chinese Medicine.

Because it was extremely difficult to grow outside of China and Tibet, for a time Chinese rhubarb was more expensive than highly prized spices such as cinnamon and nutmeg and even opium. Despite Arabian texts touting its superiority, the hybrid garden rhubarb cultivated along the Volga River gained in popularity because of its availability and lower cost. In addition to being called Russian rhubarb, the hybrid also became known as crown rhubarb because of its showy crown of leaves.

Accounts differ in regard to when this plant arrived in England. However, by the late sixteenth century, physician and botanist John Gerard wrote about the uses of rhubarb. Less than a century later, master herbalist Nicholas Culpeper raved about the plant. Among the many things attributed to American founding father Benjamin Franklin is rhubarb's hop across the Atlantic. During his stay in England, Franklin shipped seeds to his friend, naturalist John Bartram, back home in the Colonies because he thought the plant would interest him.

Well into the eighteenth century, garden rhubarb was regarded as a medicinal plant even though it wasn't a superstar healer like its Chinese cousin. That said, garden rhubarb has several good uses. The astringent and antibacterial properties of its root work well for dealing with acne, burns, and abrasions. The phytoestrogens in the root have also been found to help subdue menopausal hot flashes. Some of the other compounds in the roots and rhizomes are being studied for use in fighting Alzheimer's and other diseases.

Because the dried root of garden rhubarb is not widely available to purchase, you may want to harvest some of your own. Do it in the autumn or early spring when the plant's energy is focused in the roots, making them more potent. Rather than taking the whole root, take part of it when it is big enough to divide. Wash and scrub with water, and then cut the roots into small pieces for drying. Place paper towels on a cookie sheet and spread out the rhubarb in a single layer. Set the oven at the lowest temperature for three to four hours. Leave the door ajar to allow air circulation and to keep the roots from baking. Turn them for uniform drying. Transfer the roots to a screen and place it in a warm room to complete the drying process, which will take a week or two.

Rhubarb and Aloe Healing Gel

> 4 tablespoons dried, chopped rhubarb root
>
> 2 cups water
>
> 6–8 tablespoons aloe vera gel

Place the rhubarb root and water in a saucepan and bring to a boil. Stir, cover, and reduce the heat to as low as possible. Simmer for 20 minutes or until the liquid is reduced by at least half. Let the mixture cool completely before straining. Place the aloe gel in a bowl and slowly stir in the decoction until the mixture reaches a consistency you like. Store in a glass jar with a tight-fitting lid.

Rhubarb Hot Flash Tincture

> ¾ cup dried, chopped rhubarb root
>
> 2 cups 80–100 proof alcohol (rum, brandy, or vodka)

Place the rhubarb and alcohol in a glass jar with a tight-fitting lid. Close and shake for 1–2 minutes. Shake the jar every other day for 2–4 weeks before straining. Store in a dark glass bottle away from sunlight. Take 1 teaspoon 2–3 times a day diluted in 1 ounce of water, tea, or fruit juice.

Growing Rhubarb

Today's increasing interest in gardening and heirloom plants has boosted rhubarb's comeback. This plant is as hardy as a weed and easy to grow, and when given some attention and TLC, it will reward you with bountiful harvests for at least five years or more. Rhubarb does best in cooler regions; the dormant root crown needs temperatures below 40 degrees Fahrenheit (5 degrees Celcius) to stimulate the next cycle of growth.

Rhubarb can be started from seed, but it takes a long time for the plant to get established. Instead, purchase rhubarb crowns, which can be planted in the early spring. The crown is the top part of the root where it joins the bottom of the stems. Plant each crown in its own little mound about two inches deep. Because it does not transplant well, it's best to locate rhubarb where it will stay put. For best results, give it plenty of room (at least a square yard, or nine square feet) where it won't be disturbed.

While rhubarb thrives in full sun, it can be equally happy in partial shade. Keep the soil consistently moist, but be sure it is well-drained so it doesn't become soggy. Because rhubarb requires little or no fertilizer, a layer of compost used as mulch feeds it and helps the soil retain moisture. Mulch will also help to keep down weeds. Resist the temptation to pick stalks during the first year. The nourishment that the plant receives from the leaves will build a strong root system and ensure robust growth in the years ahead. It's hard to wait, but patience is key.

Harvesting can begin when the plant is in its second season, but go easy and just take a few stalks from each plant so it can continue generating energy to ensure future bounty.

In the past, garden rhubarb's botanical synonym, R. rhaponticum, was used for what was thought to be a separate species. It was known variously as Russian rhubarb, Siberian rhubarb, and false rhubarb.

Choose stalks that are at least ten to twelve inches long and one to two inches thick. Use a sharp knife and cut them as close to the ground as you can without damaging the root crown. Remove and discard the leaves, as they contain large amounts of oxalic acid, which is slightly toxic. Also remove flower stalks as soon as they appear by cutting them at the base. This will keep the plant's energy and growth in the roots and the edible leaf stalks.

While rhubarb is relatively trouble free, there is one particular pest to watch out for: the rhubarb curculio, also known as the rhubarb weevil. The curculio is a type of beetle that bores into the crowns, roots, and stalks of the plant. These half-inch-long bugs are particularly fond of wild dock (*Rumex crispus*), so if you have any growing in the vicinity of your garden, get rid of it because the curculio will move on to your rhubarb for the second course in its feast. Remove the bugs by hand from your plants and sprinkle a little diatomaceous earth around the base of each mound to deter them.

Beginning in its third year, rhubarb will give you an eight-to-ten-week harvest period. Even when the plants are mature, take only about a third to half of the stalks from each to keep them healthy and vigorous. Once cut, stems will keep in the refrigerator for about a week. If your plants are producing more than you need, chop and freeze some for later use. However, as I have found, friends will love you if you share.

Today, there are many varieties of garden rhubarb that accommodate a wide range of tastes. 'Canada Red' has thick red stalks and is sweeter than most varieties. 'MacDonald' is brilliant red, has tender stalks, and is a favorite for pies and freezing. 'Valentine' has more of a ruby color and is often recommended for its mild flavor and fragrant aroma. The stalks of 'Victoria' are raspberry red at the base but graduate to green at the top. They have a slightly sweet, earthy taste. Another popular variety is 'Crimson Red', with stalks that can reach between two and three feet long. It has a sweet-tart taste and is especially winter hardy.

Rhubarb Recipes

In the early 1800s, the use of rhubarb changed, and it was found more often on the dinner table than in the medicine cabinet. The stalks had not been used prior to this time until they were discovered to be a good substitute for fruit when combined with sugar, honey, or molasses. Fast forward two centuries and garden rhubarb has also become known as culinary rhubarb. Not only is there a plethora of recipes showing up online, entire cookbooks are being devoted to it, and it's even available in supermarkets.

In addition to earning a new place in the kitchen, rhubarb also ranks high among healthy foods for the diet. It contains calcium and vitamin K, which strengthens bones. With lutein and zeaxanthin, rhubarb is good for the eyes. It is high in antioxidants such as vitamin A, which is good for healthy skin, and vitamin C, which helps fight infection. Rhubarb also contains protein, potassium, and vitamin B complex. If that's not enough, it is low in calories too.

With a strong, tart flavor, rhubarb is still often prepared with a generous amount of sugar or paired with something sweet. However, it is also making an appearance in cakes, muffins, jams, and barbecued chicken sauce. Rhubarb is even used to make a vinaigrette salad dressing without vinegar. However, one of my favorites is the classic from England that my grandmother used to make: stewed rhubarb and angelica. The sweet taste of angelica offsets the tartness of rhubarb.

Traditional Rhubarb and Angelica

2 cups rhubarb stalks, sliced into ½-inch pieces

¼ cup angelica stems, finely chopped

⅓ cup sugar

2 tablespoons water

Toss the rhubarb and angelica with the sugar until they are coated. Add the water and simmer for about 10 minutes until the rhubarb is tender. Serve as a dessert, use as a pie filling, or use as a topping for ice cream or cheesecake.

Folklore

Like many plants, rhubarb has its share of folklore. Dreaming of rhubarb meant that you would get back into the good graces of someone with whom you had had a falling out. In Oxfordshire, England, the first rhubarb of the year was supposed be eaten on Easter Sunday; the reason for this is unknown. A piece of rhubarb was worn as a charm to prevent children from developing a clubfoot. A leaf applied to the forehead was said to relieve headache, and wearing a piece of rhubarb root as a pendant was said to relieve stomachache. It was also used as a remedy to strengthen fingernails, remove scabs, and relieve earaches.

According to early twentieth-century American folklorists Vance Randolph and George P. Wilson, rhubarb came to be called pie plant because in the Ozarks, the word *rhubarb* had a sexual connotation. In addition to its phallic shape, rhubarb was believed to be an aphrodisiac and a cure for erectile problems. In England and America, the word *rhubarb* has been used in slang as reference to both the penis and impotence.

About its funky name: the species name *rhabarbarum* and the shortened *rhubarb* were derived from the combination of *Rha*, the Greek name for the Volga River, an area where rhubarb was grown, and the Latin *barbarum,* meaning "foreign," which is also the source of the word *barbarian*, according to naturalist Dr. Umberto Quattrocchi.

By the mid-twentieth century, as fewer people kept herb and vegetable gardens, rhubarb seemed destined to become a thing of the past. But as often happens, what's old becomes new again. Rhubarb has even gained stature as an ornamental plant. Several varieties have been developed especially for landscaping to add a striking accent or focal point. Some of these varieties are extremely large, reaching a height of five to six feet and spreading as much as ten. Other ornamental varieties have remarkable maroon or red leaves. The ordinary garden variety is also turning up as an ornamental, even in the small public park around the corner from my house.

No matter what variety you grow, don't limit rhubarb to the garden or kitchen. Its large, frilly leaves, colorful stalks, and clouds of flowers add a dramatic touch to flower arrangements. Resembling pinkish cauliflowers in the beginning, rhubarb flowers open into billowing cream-colored clusters that float above the leaves. Of course, if you are growing rhubarb for the table, you'll want to remove the flowers so the plant puts its energy into the stalks. No matter what your purpose for growing rhubarb, it's an interesting plant that provides a great place for kids to play hide-and-seek.

Resources

Foust, Clifford M. *Rhubarb: The Wondrous Drug.* Princeton, NJ: Princeton University Press, 2014.

Lemm, Elaine. *The Great Book of Rhubarb.* Bradford, England: Great Northern Books, 2011.

Quattrocchi, Umberto. *CRC World Dictionary of Plant Names.* Vol. 4, R–Z. Boca Raton, FL: CRC Press, 2000. Page 2,294.

Randolph, Vance, and George P. Wilson. *Down in the Holler: A Gallery of Ozark Folk Speech.* Norman, OK: University of Oklahoma, 1953. Page 102.

Chamomile

→ JD Hortwort ←

If any flowering plants are over-looked in today's landscape, it's probably the ones that eventually find their way into roadside ditches and wayward places. Seriously, when was the last time you stopped to admire the sky-blue flower of a chicory plant? Or the bright, flashy orange of a cow itch trumpet flower? These are very striking flowers, if you can make a minute in your day to consider them.

Now, pity the poor chamomile with its less-than-noticeable, daisy-like flowers that are barely the size of a dime. Daisies are perhaps the most common flower shape in the Western plant world. What's one more daisy blossom on the side of the road

German Chamomile	
Species	Matricaria chamomilla
Zone	3–9
Needs	☼☼☼ 💧
Soil pH	5.5–7.5
Size	18–24 in.

in among the asters, boltonias, fleabanes, ox-eyes, and black-eyed Susans?

With its tiny yet prominent yellow eye and small rays of white petals swaying delicately over soft, ferny foliage, it's no wonder that we rarely give chamomiles a second look.

But we should.

Back in the Day

When we talk about chamomile, we are generally speaking of either Roman chamomile (*Chamaemelum nobile*) or German chamomile (*Matricaria chamomilla*). There are a lot of other herbs that have been labeled "chamomile" over the centuries including Moroccan chamomile (*Cladanthus*), yellow chamomile (*Cota tinctoria*), stinking chamomile (*Anthemis cotula*), and wild chamomile (*Tripleurospermum inodorum*). Most of these, however, don't hold a candle to the real thing.

Like our forefathers, we use German and Roman chamomile. We'll talk about the differences in a bit. The Greek *chamomaela* roughly translates to "ground apple"; the ancients noticed the plant smelled of apples when the foliage was bruised.

By the way, the ancient Greeks were probably talking about the plant we call German chamomile, which is native to most of Europe and Western Asia. Roman chamomile is native to Western Europe and North Africa. You may sometimes see Roman chamomile referred to as English chamomile or garden chamomile.

The Greeks, Egyptians, and Romans soon learned that a tea of the herb could be used for both cosmetic and medicinal needs. Hippocrates recommended it to treat colds. It was touted as a solution for inflammations wherever they occurred on the body, soothing for the nerves and calming to the stomach. Our ancestors applied it to diaper rash, canker sores, and poison ivy rash, just to mention a few uses.

It was used to flavor beer, improve the complexion and highlight the hair. On top of all that, it was encouraged to be grown as a lawn herb because walking on it was so pleasing and being trodden underfoot didn't seem to discourage the plant at all.

Who wouldn't want to have this plant around? Fortunately, growing chamomile couldn't be easier.

Get to Growing

First, you should decide which of these plants you want to grow. Both Roman and German chamomile have useful essential oils, but technically, German chamomile is considered the most medicinal because it has the highest concentration of beneficial essential oils.

German chamomile is a self-seeding annual that grows to about two feet tall and provides plenty of flowers for harvest throughout the season. You can also harvest the leaves, but it is the flowers that are generally used in teas. It is hardy from zones 3 through 9, so just about anyone in the United States should be able to grow it.

Roman chamomile is perennial and low growing, reaching roughly two to four inches in height. It is listed as hardy from zones 4 through 9, slightly less hardy than the German variety but not much so. It will flower, but the number of flowers will be fewer. This is the one popularized in medieval gardens as a lawn herb. In fact, in his play *Henry IV, Part 1,* Shakespeare has Falstaff point out when speaking of chamomile, "The more it is trodden on the faster it grows" (act 2, scene 2).

Of course, there is nothing that says you can't grow both. In my experience, the keys are well-drained soil and plenty of sun. My first efforts many years ago included seeding both types of chamomile. Frankly, I had more luck with German chamomile. The Roman variety didn't seem to respond quite as robustly. In retrospect, I think I may have been too generous with the water and the fertilizer.

Chamomile is definitely one of those herbs that doesn't like to be coddled. I used a general-purpose potting soil and, once the seedlings had germinated in about seven to ten days, I watered with a 20-20-20 liquid fertilizer (nitrogen, phosphorus, and potassium) at half strength. The seedlings were few and far between. Even with good light for growth, they were spindly. When I finally got a few sets of decent size for transplanting, most of the plants died off.

What an abundance of lessons I learned about growing chamomile! First, chamomile of both types likes lean soil. Just like humans who try to live off too much fat and sugar, chamomile plants will never reach their full potential if they are given too many nutrients. This is one of those times that using peat plugs is a better option than a seed tray. Plus, these days I leave off the fertilizer until transplanting. The second reason for using peat plugs is chamomile doesn't like to be disturbed. Shakespeare was right. You can walk all over the plant, once it is mature. But, like a petulant child, chamomile is likely to pitch a terminal fit if it is being plucked out of a seed tray.

Instead of trying to start seeds inside, for my next attempt, I directly seeded my chamomile outside in a sunny spot after all danger of frost in my area had passed. I merely loosened the soil in the planting bed and scattered the seeds on top— no need to try to bury them. The German chamomile was as happy as a clam and rewarded me with plenty of flowers over that growing season. The Roman chamomile, not so much.

This was my next lesson in chamomile culture. As a perennial, Roman chamomile is best grown from sets. Let the nursery professionals fuss over it! Once you get the plant established in your landscape, you will find that Roman chamomile will tend to root along the stems as it spreads. If you want to increase your population, it's a simple matter to snip the stem and move the new plants with a root system that is already established to a different location in the garden.

Chamomile doesn't have many pests, if it is grown in the right spot. The biggest concern comes from fungal wilt if the soil doesn't drain well or if you don't have a sunny enough spot for the plant.

As mentioned earlier, German chamomile produces the most flowers. These should be sheared from the plant while still young and fresh and dried under a low, indirect heat to preserve the essential oils. Just take a pair of scissors to the garden and cut the flowers off an inch or two below the bud. To increase the bushiness of the plant, cut the entire plant back by half. This means if the plant is eighteen inches tall after you have taken the flowers, cut it back to nine inches tall.

Roman chamomile is naturally low growing. All you should have to do with it is keep the flowers cut as they are produced.

Once you have mastered growing chamomiles, you will find an abundance of uses for it, from the garden to the medicine cabinet to the boudoir.

In the Garden

Chamomiles make great companion plants. We plant certain plants together because of the benefits they give each other. For example, the apple-y fragrance that we love so much in chamomile is obnoxious to many insects. So when you plant chamomile with cabbage, broccoli, and cauliflower, you ward away pesky thrips and aphids. Chamomile flowers will also attract parasite wasps that prey on caterpillars and other damaging insects. Brassicas love chamomile, but, honestly, you can interplant it with any flower or vegetable.

You know about chamomile tea for people, but did you know it is good for plants too? It is a natural source of organic sulfur. You can brew a strong tea of the leaves and tops and use the resulting liquid as a first line defense against plant fungus and bacteria.

Boil 4 cups of water and add ½ cup dried chamomile. Let the tea brew for at least 20 minutes. Once it has cooled, use it at full strength on any plant that you are worried about developing a problem with mildew or mold.

You can also use the tea to presoak any seed with a hard coat. You may have seen advice to presoak nasturtium, morning glory, and okra seeds to ensure good germination. If you do the soak with a chamomile tea, you will also be providing the seed with protection from dampening off. Don't be afraid to use a cool chamomile tea to water any seedlings you have germinated to prevent the same issues.

In the Medicine Cabinet

As mentioned earlier, chamomile has always been considered a "must-have" herb for the medicine cabinet. However, you should be aware of a few concerns.

The experts at WebMD.com remind people that, if they are allergic to any plant in the aster family (such as ragweed or chrysanthemum), they may experience an allergic reaction to chamomile. This is true whether you are drinking the tea or applying a tincture to some part of your body.

Use of the tea should be stopped two weeks before surgery. Be aware that drinking large amounts of the tea could cause an interaction with blood-thinning medications and some painkillers. There is conflicting information, but as a general rule, giving any herbal tea to an infant under six months of age is not recommended.

With that said, this herb can be said to be a general cure-all for life's bothersome afflictions. Have a cold? Not only will drinking a warm cup of chamomile tea make you feel better, but inhaling the steam will improve your breathing. The warm tea is also a good gargle for a sore throat, after dental work, and for inflamed gums.

There is hardly a television show or movie during which at some point one character doesn't turn to a distraught friend and say, "You look like you could use a cup of chamomile tea." The tea is sedating. Even breathing the fumes from a cuddled cup of chamomile tea can help ease mild depression, experts tell us.

I personally like to blend equal amounts of chamomile and perilla if I have an occasional bout of sleeplessness. I find that the apple flavor of the chamomile blends perfectly with the warm anise flavor of the perilla to make a great sleepy-time tea. Chamomile is also known to calm menstrual cramps in women, relieve gas, and help with tension headaches.

As a wash, the tea can help keep wounds from infection. It has been used as a sitz bath for relief from hemorrhoids and as a treatment for vaginitis. It may also have benefits in the treatment of eczema, but more study is needed in this area.

In the Boudoir

As if all this were not enough to encourage you to grow your own chamomile, there are beauty benefits too. The same tea that helps get you through a bout of the cold can help control acne when applied as a rinse. Simply brew a standard cup of the tea, and, when it has cooled, use a cotton ball to apply to the affected area after washing. Even if you don't have acne, an evening rinse with chamomile tea at the end of the day can be refreshing and rejuvenating for your skin.

A strong chamomile tea can revive dull blonde hair and give golden highlights to brown hair when used regularly. Use ½ cup of dried flowers to 6 cups of boiling water. After adding the herb to the water, reduce the heat and simmer for 20 minutes. Let the mixture cool to a tepid temperature. Strain it and use the strong tea on clean, wet hair. Thoroughly soak your hair and, if possible, let the mixture stay for an hour before rinsing. This treatment may take 2–3 applications before you see results, but it has also been found to help cover up those first signs of gray.

Garden aide, cure-all, beauty treatment—how many herbs can claim to do all of that? The simple little chamomile, cultured for thousands of years, is still proving its worth in our modern world.

Selected Resources

Johnson, Jackie. "23 Ways to Use Chamomile." Herbal Academy. July 13, 2015. https://theherbalacademy.com/23-ways-to-use-chamomile/.

Srivastava, Janmejai K., and Eswar Shankar, and Sanjay Gupta. "Chamomile: A Herbal Medicine of the Past with a Bright Future." *Molecular Medicine Reports* 3, no. 6 (November 2010): 895–901. doi:10.3892/mmr.2010.377.

Villines, Zawn. "What Are the Benefits of Chamomile Tea?" Medical News Today. Last modifed November 15, 2017. https://www.medicalnewstoday.com/articles/320031.php.

Comfrey

⇜ Rachael Witt ⇝

My first introduction to comfrey was at the entrance to a community garden. I remember walking through a dense colony of bristly-haired plants and then being asked to remove them from the pathway. I spent the entire day digging up the thick, branching taproots and setting them aside to later experiment with their medicinal uses. Weeks later, I had a batch of rancid infused oil, and clusters of young leaves had emerged alongside the pathway. Little did I know, comfrey had a lot to teach me.

Comfrey, *Symphytum officinale*, is an herbaceous perennial in the borage family. It is wildly rooted in Europe and Asia and a garden escapee found throughout most of North

Comfrey	
Species	*Symphytum officinale*
Zone	3–9
Needs	☀☀ 💧💧
Soil pH	6.0–7.0
Size	2–3 ft., up & out

America. This prolific plant can be mowed down, dug up, and chewed out by a weed-whacker, and it will come back stronger than before.

Comfrey in the Garden

Comfrey begins growing young leaves from old plant crowns or from its wide-spreading taproots. In early spring, its large, oblong- to oval-shaped leaves extend from winged petioles.

These basal leaves have rough hairs on both sides and smooth leaf edges. Smaller leaves without petioles alternately grow up a flowering stem shortly thereafter. By early summer, the buzzing of bees is a sound way of finding comfrey in flower. Bell-shaped, yellowish-white to pinkish-purple flowering clusters uncoil at the branching tips of a stem.

Though comfrey is a character that spreads beyond its boundaries, it is favored by many gardeners for attracting pollinators and serving as a ground cover, fertilizer, and animal fodder. Comfrey is high in vitamins A, C, and B_{12} and an excellent source of potassium, nitrogen, and phosphorous.

To harvest comfrey, use garden shears, a sickle, or a scythe to cut at the base of the leaves or flowering stalk. The aerial parts of the plant can be harvested several times throughout the summer. The roots are best harvested in the fall and winter. Use a spade or garden fork to loosen the soil around the roots, and then use the spade or pruners to cut the branching roots. Remember, comfrey grows well with disturbance and the roots are hard to eradicate. To further propagate comfrey, use two-to-six-inch root cuttings and plant horizontally two to six inches deep. Once established, comfrey will take care of itself.

When harvesting comfrey, you might experience "slime" exuding from its stalk: this is the mucilaginous part of the plant that refers to comfrey's demulcent properties. It's moisturizing, soothing, and outright comforting. Comfrey lubricates both the gastrointestinal tract and the respiratory tract, and externally soothes inflammation, burns, wounds, and skin irritations.

Comfrey Compost Tea

Comfrey bioaccumulates nutrients and minerals with its long taproots. This makes the whole plant a rich natural fertilizer. Harvested aerial parts of comfrey can be laid on top of garden beds, around trees and perennial shrubs, in a compost bin, or steeped into compost tea. To further boost nitrogen, phosphorus, and potassium in your soil, try this tea technique plants love.

Loosely fill a 5-gallon bucket (or barrel) about ¾ full with freshly cut comfrey.

Add water to fill the bucket (or barrel). Cover it with a lid and let it steep for 3–6 weeks.

Dilute the compost tea by ½ or more. Apply the liquid to the base of plants. Use the broken-down plant matter at the bottom of the bucket to activate compost or mulch the base of trees.

Healing with Comfrey

Comfrey is also known as knitbone and has a reputation as a wound healer. It has been used to heal torn skin, broken bones, fractures, and sprains as well as strengthen ligaments and tendons. The whole plant contains the constituent allantoin, which causes cell proliferation that increases the healing of wounds, both inside and out and from top to bottom. Take care to apply comfrey on closed or clean wounds because the rapid growth of tissues can trap bacteria and possibly cause infection.

While comfrey is nourishing and extremely healing, it is said to be a controversial plant because it contains pyrrolizidine alkaloids that can cause liver disease in humans. This alkaloid is most prevalent in the roots yet is also found in early spring leaves. Some people continue to use comfrey internally as needed and avoid prolonged high doses, while others have stopped using the plant altogether. In spite of this, comfrey may safely be used externally by everyone.

Comfrey Poultice

There are many ways to make a poultice. The most basic, simple, go-to poultice that I use is called a spit poultice. Yes, I use spit as a healing agent. Yet this poultice recipe is for a larger quantity of herbs and is something to be stored in the freezer for future injuries.

Comfrey poultices are used for pain relief and to reduce inflammation, swelling, and bruising. This poultice can be used on breaks and sprains to help mend tissues and increase the rate of recovery.

6 large leaves of comfrey (or 1 flowering stalk)

½ cup warm water (or ¼ cup water and 5 ice cubes)

2 tablespoons herbal infused oil or flax seeds (optional)

Harvest fresh plant material and cut or tear it into your blender or food processor. Pour warm water (or ice and cold water if you want a cold poultice) over plant material. Blend until it becomes a soft, mushy paste. Add herbal infused oil (I highly recommend calendula oil or arnica oil, depending on the injury) or flax seeds to make it gel and increase the medicinal strength of your poultice.

Blend. Apply the poultice directly to skin or place it in the center of a bandana or clean cloth, folding in the poultice and then applying it to the injury. Keep the poultice on the injury for 15–20 minutes.

Toward the end of fall, I make a large batch of comfrey poultice to store for the winter. I spoon out enough poultice onto a clean cloth so that when I fold it, the cloth and poultice will fit into a sandwich bag. Instead of using an ice pack, I will use my frozen comfrey poultice on injuries that are swollen and painful. The frozen comfrey poultice can keep up to 2 months.

Infused Comfrey Oil

Comfrey is a mucilaginous plant that is both soothing and cooling. It makes for a great topical remedy for burns, closed wounds, skin irritations, rashes, dryness, and inflammation.

Since the mucilage is water dense, it makes the plant difficult to infuse into an oil base. Infused oils can be stored for a great length of time when kept in a cool, dark place with minimal contact with air, moisture, heat, and light. Depending on the smell and the color of the oil, some oils can maintain potency for one to three years.

Hence, when I first experimented with infusing comfrey into an oil, I ended up with fowl-smelling, rancid oil. Comfrey is great at teaching us how to infuse a moist plant into an oil-based menstruum. After much trial and error, I have found a few methods that work well. Here are two techniques to make a comfrey infused oil:

Heat Method

    1 part wilted comfrey leaves (and flowers)

    5 parts carrier oil (Olive oil, grapeseed oil, and sesame oil are recommended, yet almond oil and castor oil can also be used for skin care.)

Wilt the freshly harvested comfrey plant for 12 hours (do not dry it). Chop and mash the wilted comfrey to a fine pulp. Place the mashed material into an apparatus with a thermostatic control that allows you to maintain a temperature between 100°F and 130°F. (A yogurt maker, slow cooker, pilot light in oven, or hot pad can all function as heating elements as long as they do not exceed 130°F.)

Pour a carrier oil of your choice over the mashed comfrey. Stir the mixture well, making sure that all the comfrey material is covered with the oil. Carrier oils are generally fixed oils that are soluble with volatile oils. Good carrier oils to start with include olive oil, grapeseed oil, sunflower oil, coconut oil, and sesame oil. Since some oils pose an allergy risk, I recommend starting with a hypoallergenic oil such as olive oil.

Leave the comfrey and oil mixture uncovered on low heat (ideally 100°F) for a couple of days. Keeping the infusion uncovered will allow moisture to evaporate from the oil. After a few days, I will cover the mixture with a muslin cloth or lid and allow it to infuse for up to 10 days and nights, stirring every day.

If the oil begins to smell like something is going "off" or starting to ferment, increase the heat to 150°F for a few hours. This will eliminate any opportunistic organisms that produce fermentation. Do not keep the oil at such a high temperature because it can burn both the comfrey and the oil.

When the oil is a dark green, almost black color and smells more "herbal," your infusion is complete. While the oil is warm, use a strainer to separate the oil and comfrey leaves and press the remaining pulp.

To further prevent rancidity, pour the oil infusion into a clear glass jar, cover the top with a lid, and allow it to sit for another 4–5 days. The water impurities will settle to the bottom of the jar, leaving the pure oil at the top. Gently pour off the top oil into another glass container. Discard the water impurities and other plant material that settled at the bottom. Keep an eye on the final product for a couple more days to ensure that there are no more water impurities in the oil.

When oil is clear, pour into an airtight glass bottle; label with the name of the herb (Comfrey, *Symphytum officinale*), oil type, date, and uses. Store in a cool, dark place. A refrigerator or freezer can prolong the shelf life of your oil, as long as no moisture and minimal air exposure occurs.

Dried Method

1 part dried powdered comfrey

5 parts carrier oil

Harvest comfrey leaves and dry them in a dehydrator until crisp. Grind the dried comfrey to a fine powder. Place powdered comfrey into a jar that can hold the comfrey-oil ratio. Pour carrier oil over powdered comfrey and stir the mixture well. Then, cap the jar tightly and shake to further mix the comfrey and oil.

Dried herbs will absorb the oil within a day of mixing the two together. Check your comfrey and oil mixture the following day and add extra oil if absorption occurred. Place the jar in a warm location out of direct light to infuse for 7–10 days, shaking the mixture as much as possible.

The infusion will be a dark green, almost black color when it is completed. Decant the oil by straining out the powdered comfrey with a muslin cloth and strainer. Let the decanted oil sit for a couple more days, allowing more sediment to rest at bottom of the jar. Strain one more time. Bottle in an airtight glass container; label with the name of the herb (Comfrey, *Symphytum officinale*), oil type, date, and uses.

Comfy Comfrey Salve

This recipe is for an all-purpose healing salve that is great for closed wounds, skin rashes and irritations, burns, inflammation, and tissue mending.

   1 cup comfrey infused oil

   ⅓ cup calendula infused oil

   ⅓ cup arnica infused oil

   ⅓ cup St. John's wort infused oil

   2 ounces beeswax

   Small glass jars or tins

Combine infused oils in a pot or double boiler. Over very low heat (if using a double boiler, higher heat is okay), warm up the oils and add the beeswax to the mix. Stir occasionally until the beeswax melts. As the beeswax is melting, set up small glass jars or tins for the salve to set in.

Test the consistency of the salve by dipping a tablespoon into the mixture and setting it on a plate. Place the spoon and plate in the freezer until the mixture cools. Check the firmness of the salve to see if it is the consistency you like. For a harder slave, add more beeswax. For a softer salve, add more oil. Once the mixture reaches the optimal consistency, take the pot off the heat and pour into the small glass jars or tins. Once the salve has solidified, place lids on the containers. Store them in a cool, dark place.

Salves can last for up to 1 year (sometimes more, if stored in an airtight container in the freezer), unless they are kept in the car or warm places and used often, causing deterioration.

Comfrey Aloe Gel

This external remedy was inspired by Rosemary Gladstar. I used this gel when I was recovering from a severe back injury. Applied topically, it helped relieve swelling and inflammation while rapidly reducing the recovery time of torn tissues and broken bones. It is also known to alleviate arthritic joints and sore muscles.

¼ cup dried comfrey roots (or ½ cup freshly chopped roots)

1 quart water

¼ cup aloe gel

1 teaspoon cayenne powder

1–2 drops peppermint essential oil

1–2 drops camphor essential oil

1–2 drops wintergreen essential oil

Make comfrey root decoction by adding dried roots and 1 quart water into a pot. Heat on low until water comes to a simmer. Cover pot and let roots simmer for 25–45 minutes. For stronger decoctions, let simmer for a longer time or let the simmered roots infuse in the water overnight. Strain comfrey root and combine ¼ cup comfrey decoction with aloe gel, cayenne powder, and essential oils. Mix well. Store in a glass jar in the refrigerator for up to 7 days.

Apply liberally over inflamed areas or injuries.

Comfrey heals, soothes, and nourishes. It is a strong plant that brings beauty, wellness, and biodiversity. May this article inspire you to learn more and experiment with the herbal gifts of comfrey.

Resources

Alfrey, Paul. "Comfrey: Its History, Uses & Benefits." *Permaculture Magazine*, March 3, 2016. www.permaculture.co.uk/articles /comfrey-its-history-uses-benefits.

Gladstar, Rosemary. *Rosemary Gladstar's Medicinal Herbs: A Beginner's Guide*. North Adams, MA: Storey Publishing, 2012.

Green, James. *The Herbal Medicine-Makers' Handbook: A Home Manual*. New York: Crossing Press, 2000.

Grieve, Maude. "Comfrey." A Modern Herbal (Botanical.com). 1995. botanical.com/botanical/mgmh/c/comfre92.html.

Hoffmann, David. *The New Holistic Herbal: A Herbal Celebrating the Wholeness of Life*. New York: Barnes & Noble, 1995.

Kloos, Scott. *Pacific Northwest Medicinal Plants: Identify, Harvest, and Use 120 Wild Herbs for Health and Wellness*. Portland, OR: Timber Press, 2017.

Skenderi, Gazmend. *Herbal Vade Mecum: 800 Herbs, Spices, Essential Oils, Lipids, Etc., Constituents, Properties, Uses, and Caution*. Futherford, NJ: Herbacy Press, 2003.

Tierra, Lesley. *Healing with the Herbs of Life*. New York: Crossing Press, 2003.

Sunflower

✤ Susan Pesznecker ✤

Mention the word *sunflower* and most folks immediately picture an enormous, stately flower with a bright gold blossom about twelve inches across and a stalk that many feet high. This is no exaggeration, either. Even with no tending, the common sunflower can reach spectacular heights: at this year's Oregon State Fair, the winning sunflower passed sixteen feet! These majestic flowers mirror the brilliant sun, and the young plants actually follow the sun as their flowers begin to show, tracking the solar arc through the sky.

Speaking of "following the sun," conventional lore claims that fully grown sunflowers actually rotate through the day, following the sun's

Sunflower	
Species	*Helianthus annuus*
Zone	2–11
Needs	☀️☀️💧
Soil pH	6.0–7.5
Size	up to 15 ft.

movements. This isn't completely correct, though. In truth, it's the young plants that actually follow the sun, and this mostly happens before they begin to bloom. Once the flowers are in bloom, they tend to remain fixed in place, and the mature flowers of the common sunflower generally face east, toward the sunrise.

According to Greek mythology, Clytie, a nymph, loved the god Apollo (in some versions, Helios). Apollo originally returned Clytie's love but then fell in love with Leucothoe and threw Clytie away. This is where it gets good . . . A jealous Clytie retaliated by going to Leucothoe's father and informing him that his daughter was doing the deed with Apollo. Dear old dad punished Leucothoe by burying her alive. A little extreme, right? Enter Apollo, so furious with Clytie that he turned her into—you guessed it—a large golden flower. Doomed to her new life as foliage, flower-Clytie would still watch her beloved Apollo each day as he rode his chariot across the sky, and, thus, the sunflower legend took shape.

The flower's seed head demonstrates a version of the Fibonacci spiral or sequence, a mathematical pattern that often appears in nature. The seed pattern also approximates the "golden ratio," meaning that our common sunflower has something in common with the Pyramids of Giza, da Vinci's Mona Lisa, and Ptolemy's theorem.

All sunflowers are a type of aster, or daisy, coming from the family Asteraceae and belonging to the genus *Helianthus,* which has some seventy species of flowering plants, each sporting variations in size, shape, and color. Colors may vary from golden yellows to reds, oranges, and browns and from solid colors to streaks and whorls. The genus has its origins in the Americas but has since been carried to other countries as well.

The common megasunflower carries the scientific name of *Helianthus annuus*, literally a *sun*flower. The common sunflower resembles the sun via its dinner-plate–size seed head and even larger frame of golden petals. It's an annual plant, meaning the flowers grow from seed each spring and die completely back at the end of the season. Thankfully, the plants produce so many seeds that their regeneration is rarely in doubt—especially with help from the local squirrels, who invariably "squirrel away" enough sunflower seeds to ensure the next year's crop.

The Jerusalem artichoke or "sunchoke" (*Helianthus tuberosus*) is another well-known sunflower. Other species may be named for location (California sunflower or southeastern sunflower) or given descriptive names (showy sunflower, neglected sunflower, or alkali sunflower). A few bear the names of those who discovered or nurtured them, like Smith's and Porter's sunflowers. Different species are found in both annual and perennial versions. Wild-growing sunflower species are often threatened by development and deforestation, and some of the perennial versions may become invasive if not controlled.

Growing Your Own

To grow your own common sunflowers, plant the seeds in rich, well-drained soil in a sunny location after frost danger has passed. Water occasionally; they don't love their feet to be too wet, but they appreciate a moist bed. Sunflowers will tolerate a great deal of heat and a certain amount of drought, making them ideal for novice gardeners. Once the flowers begin to gain height, the stalks may need to be supported, and occasional feeding with a good plant food could help you raise your own state-fair contender.

For even more fun on a collective level, take part in the annual International Sunflower Guerrilla Gardening Day, occurring every year on May 1. **Guerilla gardening** is the act of surreptitiously planting seeds or starts in locations that are untended, ignored, or even mistreated: parking strips, vacant lots, and highway edges are favored examples. On International Sunflower Guerrilla Gardening Day, sunflower seeds are planted in such locations. Several weeks or months later, the resulting display will brighten the lives of passers-by, while the act of planting (and maybe tending) also provides a kind of horticultural therapy, known to relieve stress.

Uses

Many people grow sunflowers simply as gorgeous garden ornaments, but the plants have other important uses and are, in fact, tremendously versatile:

- The seeds can be used as-is to feed birds, and the seeds and shells can be crushed for livestock forage.

- The seeds also provide a vitamin E and protein-rich food source for humans and qualify as a "superfood," whether used as intact or ground seeds, seed butter, or pressed cooking oil.

- The Jerusalem artichoke is a perennial plant producing small yellow flowers and tiny seeds. Its main usable product is its edible tubers, with a taste and consistency much like that of potatoes.

- The seeds may also be ground into flour and mixed with grain flours for baking or used in a sunflower variation of the sesame treat *halvah*.

- The oil, typically obtained from the smaller black seeds of certain *Helianthus* species, has culinary, cosmetic, bio-diesel, and industrial uses.

- The heart-healthy oil is high in monounsaturated fats and has a high burning temperature, making it ideal for cooking and frying.

- The petals and oil may be used for medicinal purposes, while the petals alone can be used to create infusions for medicinal uses or for dyes.

- Some varieties produce latex, which can be made into rubber.

- Sunflowers are also used today for phytoremediation, a process by which certain plants are grown in specific areas for the purpose of removing toxins—including heavy metals, radioactive materials, and other contaminants—from the soil. Recently, sunflowers were employed for this purpose at the site of the Fukushima nuclear disaster.

- Sunflowers attract bees and other pollinators. This is always important but particularly so today, with honeybees suffering from colony collapse disorder and diminishing in numbers. Something like 70 to 80 percent of the world's crops depend on pollinators, so anything we can do to support bees is important.

Feasting on Sunflowers

Roasted Sunflower Seeds

To roast sunflower seeds, start by salting them. Place the seeds in a bowl and add enough water to cover. Stir in ½ cup salt and allow to sit for several hours or overnight. Drain well, pat dry, and spread in a single layer on cookie sheets lined with silicone mats or sheets of parchment. Roast at 300°F for 30–40 minutes, stirring occasionally. For even more flavor? Toss them with olive oil first and stir with your desired sweet seasonings (e.g., cinnamon, pumpkin pie spice, ginger) or savory seasonings (red pepper flakes, chili powder, cumin), then roast as above.

You can use sunflower seeds—raw or toasted—to replace other kinds of seeds in various recipes:

- Include sunflower seeds in granola.

- For a rich, nutty flavor, add seeds to the dough when making yeast bread, use the seeds to decorate the loaves before baking, or both.

- Likewise, stir sunflower seeds into the batter for quick breads or sprinkle atop muffins, scones, or loaves for a beautiful and tasty topping.

- Make sunflower butter and jelly sandwiches.

- Scatter the seeds atop hummus and drizzle with a good olive oil.

- Garnish cooked vegetables with a toss of roasted seeds for both flavor and texture.

- Get a little crazy and sprinkle roasted seeds on tacos and quesadillas.

- Scatter a handful of roasted seeds over a bowl of soup.

- Use a coffee or spice grinder to grind roasted sunflower seeds to a coarse flour; use a 1:1 mixture of sunflower flour and panko crumbs as a breading for pan- or deep-frying.

- Replace the traditional pine nuts with sunflower seeds for a wonderful pesto—or combine both.

- Add to drop cookies—such as peanut butter or chocolate chip—for nutty flavor and a satisfying texture.

- Add raw sunflower seeds to "crisp" mixtures, such as apple crisp.

- Substitute sunflower seeds for peanuts or other nuts in your favorite nut brittle recipe.

Sprout sunflowers on a damp paper towel to create sunflower microgreens. The sprouts make perfect additions to a salad or sandwich and also make a beautiful garnish.

Sunflower Oil

Making your own sunflower oil is a fun activity for a weekend day. You'll need black oil sunflower seeds, and 3 pounds of seeds will make ½–1 quart of oil. Grind the seeds in a blender until a coarse meal results, and spread the meal on a baking sheet. Roast in a 300°F oven for 20 minutes, stirring every 5 minutes. Strain into a heat-resistant jar. If desired, strain the oil a second time through a fine mesh sieve. Cool to room temperature, then place in the refrigerator. Use within a month. (Note: the leftover solid mash can be offered to your local birds—they will be grateful!)

Sunflower oil is useful in the kitchen:

- Use sunflower oil for all frying purposes. Its high smoking point makes it ideal for this.

- Use sunflower oil to make a delicious homemade mayonnaise or aioli or as the oil component in oil and vinegar salad dressings.

- For a tasty and crispy result, replace the butter in Hasselback potatoes with sunflower oil.

As you can see, sunflower seeds and oils are incredibly versatile in the kitchen. For more ideas and a host of recipes, visit the National Sunflower Association website at www.sunflower nsa.com.

Fun with Sunflowers

When petals begin to drop off, cover the flower heads with paper bags, cheesecloth, or fine netting to keep birds and squirrels away. The seeds will ripen in thirty to forty-five days. Cut the heads from the stem and rub the seeds loose over a clean sheet or towel. Allow them to dry at room temperature for a few days before roasting or storing. If you're feeling kindly toward your feathered friends, save the dried heads until winter, then hang them from a tree and watch the feast begin!

Once bloomed, sunflowers may be cut for indoor display. Cut sunflowers in the morning to display in vases. A chopstick attached to the stems will help keep heavy flower heads from drooping.

Try your hand at painting sunflowers. You won't be the first: many artists have captured sunflowers' beauty, most notably Vincent van Gogh.

Steep a handful of petals in one to two cups boiling water to create a deep yellow dye for fabric, yarn, basket components, hard-cooked eggs, or whatever suits your fancy. Add a spoonful of white vinegar to the dye solution to help set the color.

Sunflower stalks can be harvested, dried, and cut into lengths to use as kindling. The dried stalks are quite strong and also make excellent garden poles, teepees, and trellises.

Resources

Greipsson, Sigurdur. "Phytoremediation." The Nature Education Knowledge Project, 2001. https://www.nature.com/scitable/knowledge/library/phytoremediation-17359669/.

"Recipes." National Sunflower Association. Accessed March 9, 2020. https://www.sunflowernsa.com/health/Recipes/.

Gardening Resources

Companion Planting Guide

Group together plants that complement each other by deterring certain pests, absorbing different amounts of nutrients from the soil, shading their neighbors, and enhancing friends' flavors. This table of herbs and common garden vegetables offers suggestions for plants to pair together and plants to keep separated.

Plant	Good Pairing	Poor Pairing
Anise	Coriander	Carrot, basil, rue
Asparagus	Tomato, parsley, basil, lovage, Asteraceae spp.	
Basil	Tomato, peppers, oregano, asparagus	Rue, sage, anise
Beans	Tomato, carrot, cucumber, cabbage, corn, cauliflower, potato	Gladiola, fennel, *Allium* spp.
Bee balm	Tomato, echinacea, yarrow, catnip	
Beet	Onions, cabbage, lettuce, mint, catnip, kohlrabi, lovage	Pole bean, field mustard
Bell pepper	Tomato, eggplant, coriander, basil	Kohlrabi
Borage	Tomato, squash, strawberry	
Broccoli	Aromatics, beans, celery, potato, onion, oregano, pennyroyal, dill, sage, beet	Tomato, pole bean, strawberry, peppers
Cabbage	Mint, sage, thyme, tomato, chamomile, hyssop, pennyroyal, dill, rosemary, sage	Strawberry, grape, tomato
Carrot	Peas, lettuce, chive, radish, leek, onion, sage, rosemary, tomato	Dill, anise, chamomile

Plant	Good Pairing	Poor Pairing
Catnip	Bee balm, cucumber, chamomile, mint	
Celery	Leek, tomato, bush bean, cabbage, cauliflower, carrot, garlic	Lovage
Chamomile	Peppermint, beans, peas, onion, cabbage, cucumber, catnip, dill, tomato, pumpkin, squash	
Chervil	Radish, lettuce, broccoli	
Chive	Carrot, *Brassica* spp., tomato, parsley	Bush bean, potato, peas, soybean
Coriander/ cilantro	*Plant anywhere*	Fennel
Corn	Potato, beans, peas, melon, squash, pumpkin, sunflower, soybean, cucumber	Quack grass, wheat, straw, tomato
Cucumber	Beans, cabbage, radish, sunflower, lettuce, broccoli, squash, corn, peas, leek, nasturtium, onion	Aromatic herbs, sage, potato, rue
Dill	Cabbage, lettuce, onion, cucumber	Carrot, caraway, tomato
Echinacea	Bee balm	
Eggplant	Catnip, green beans, lettuce, kale, redroot pigweed	
Fennel	*Isolate; disliked by all garden plants*	
Garlic	Tomato, rose	Beans, peas
Hyssop	*Most plants*	Radish
Kohlrabi	Green bean, onion, beet, cucumber	Tomato, strawberry, pole bean
Lavender	*Plant anywhere*	
Leek	Onion, celery, carrot, celeriac	Bush bean, soy bean, pole bean, pea

Plant	Good Pairing	Poor Pairing
Lemon balm	*All vegetables*, particularly squash, pumpkin	
Lettuce	Strawberry, cucumber, carrot, radish, dill	Pole bean, tomato
Lovage	*Most plants*, especially cucumber, beans, beet, *Brassica* spp., onion, leek, potato, tomato	Celery
Marjoram	*Plant anywhere*	
Melon	Corn, peas, morning glory	Potato, gourd
Mint	Cabbage, tomato, nettle	Parsley, rue
Nasturtium	Cabbage, cucumber, potato, pumpkin, radish	
Onion	Beets, chamomile, carrot, lettuce, strawberry, tomato, kohlrabi, summer savory	Peas, beans, sage
Oregano	*Most plants*	
Parsley	Tomato, asparagus, carrot, onion, rose	Mint, *Allium* spp.
Parsnip	Peas	
Peas	Radish, carrot, corn, cucumbers, bean, tomato, spinach, turnip, aromatic herbs	*Allium* spp., gladiola
Potato	Beans, corn, peas, cabbage, eggplant, catnip, horseradish, watermelon, nasturtium, flax	Pumpkin, raspberry, sunflower, tomato, orach, black walnut, cucumber, squash
Pumpkin	Corn, lemon balm	Potato
Radish	Peas, lettuce, nasturtium, chervil, cucumber	Hyssop
Rose	Rue, tomato, garlic, parsley, tansy	*Any plant within 1 ft. radius*
Rosemary	Rue, sage	

Plant	Good Pairing	Poor Pairing
Sage	Rosemary	Rue, onion
Spinach	Strawberry, garlic	
Squash	Nasturtium, corn, mint, catnip, radish, borage, lemon balm	Potato
Strawberry	Borage, bush bean, spinach, rue, lettuce	*Brassica* spp., garlic, kohlrabi
Tarragon	*Plant anywhere*	
Thyme	*Plant anywhere*	
Tomato	Asparagus, parsley, chive, onion, carrot, marigold, nasturtium, bee balm, nettle, garlic, celery, borage	Black walnut, dill, fennel, potato, *Brassica* spp., corn
Turnip	Peas, beans, brussels sprout, leek	Potato, tomato
Yarrow	*Plant anywhere*, especially with medicinal herbs	

For more information on companion planting, you may wish to consult the following resources:

Mayer, Dale. *The Complete Guide to Companion Planting: Everything You Need to Know to Make Your Garden Successful*. Ocala, FL: Atlantic Publishing, 2010.

Philbrick, Helen. *Companion Plants and How to Use Them*. Edinburgh, UK: Floris Books, 2016.

Riotte, Louise. *Carrots Love Tomatoes: Secrets of Companion Planting for Successful Gardening*. Pownal, VT: Storey Books, 1988.

Cooking with Herbs and Spices

Elevate your cooking with herbs and spices. Remember, a little goes a long way!

Herb	Flavor Pairings	Health Benefits
Anise	Salads, slaws, roasted vegetables	Reduces nausea, gas, and bloating. May relieve infant colic. May help menstrual pain. Loosens sputum in respiratory illnesses.
Basil	Pesto and other pasta sauces, salads	Eases stomach cramps, nausea, indigestion, and colic. Mild sedative action.
Borage	Soups	Soothes respiratory congestion. Eases sore, inflamed skin. Mild diuretic properties.
Cayenne	Adds a spicy heat to soups, sauces, and main courses	Stimulates blood flow. Relieves joint and muscle pain. Treats gas and diarrhea.
Chamomile	Desserts, teas	Used for nausea, indigestion, gas pains, bloating, and colic. Relaxes tense muscles. Eases menstrual cramps. Promotes relaxation and sleep.
Chervil	Soups, salads, and sauces	Settles and supports digestion. Mild diuretic properties. Useful in treating minor skin irritations.
Chive	Salads, potato dishes, sauces	Rich in antioxidants. May benefit insomnia. Contributes to strong bones.
Coriander/ cilantro	Soups, picante sauces, salsas	Treats mild digestive disorders. Counters nervous tensions. Sweetens breath.

Herb	Flavor Pairings	Health Benefits
Dill	Cold salads and fish dishes	Treats all types of digestive disorders, including colic. Sweetens breath. Mild diuretic.
Echinacea	Teas	Supports immune function. May treat or prevent infection.
Fennel	Salads, stir-fry, vegetable dishes	Settles stomach pain, relieves bloating, and stimulates appetite. May help treat kidney stones and bladder infections. Mild expectorant. Eye wash treats conjunctivitis.
Garlic	All types of meat and vegetable dishes as well as soup stocks and bone broths	Antiseptic: aids in wound healing. Treats and may prevent infections. Benefits the heart and circulatory system.
Ginger	Chicken, pork, stir-fry, gingerbread and ginger cookies	Treats all types of digestive disorders. Stimulates circulation. Soothes colds and flu.
Hyssop	Chicken, pasta sauces, light soups	Useful in treating respiratory problems and bronchitis. Expectorant. Soothes the digestive tract.
Jasmine	Chicken dishes, fruit desserts	Relieves tension and provides mild sedation. May be helpful in depression. Soothes dry or sensitive skin.
Lavender	Chicken, fruit dishes, ice cream	Soothes and calms the nerves. Relieves indigestion, gas, and colic. May relax airways in asthma.

Herb	Flavor Pairings	Health Benefits
Lemon balm	Soups, sauces, seafood dishes	Soothes and calms the nerves. Treats mild anxiety and depression. Helps heal wounds.
Lemongrass	Marinades, stir-fries, curries, spice rubs	Treats all types of digestive disorders. Reduces fever. May reduce pain.
Lemon verbena	Beverages, any recipe asking for lemon zest	Calms digestive problems and treats stomach pain. Gently sedative.
Lovage	Soups, lovage pesto, lentils	Acts as a digestive and respiratory tonic. Has diuretic and antimicrobial actions. Boosts circulation. Helps menstrual pain.
Marigold	Soups, salads, rice dishes	Effective treatment of minor wounds, insect bites, sunburn, acne, and other skin irritations. Benefits menstrual pain and excessive bleeding.
Marjoram	Vegetables, soups, tomato dishes, sausages	Calms the digestive system. Stimulates appetite.
Nasturtium	Nasturtium pesto, salad dressings, salads	Strong antibiotic properties. Treats wounds and respiratory infections.
Oregano	Chicken, tomato sauces and dishes	Strong antiseptic properties. Stimulates bile production. Eases flatulence.
Parsley	Soups, stocks, bone broths	Highly nutritious. Strong diuretic action and may help treat cystitis. Benefits gout, rheumatism, and arthritis.
Peppermint	Desserts, teas	Treats all types of digestive disorders. May help headaches.

Herb	Flavor Pairings	Health Benefits
Purslane	Salads	Treats digestive and bladder ailments. Mild antibiotic effects.
Rosemary	Roasted red meats, potato dishes, grilled foods	Stimulates circulation. May stimulate the adrenal glands. Elevates mood and may benefit depression.
Sage	Chicken, duck, and pork	Relieves pain in sore throats. May help treat menstrual and menopausal disorders.
Spinach	Sautéed, soups, salads, spinach pesto, stuffed in chicken, ravioli	Iron-rich; supports healthy blood and iron stores.
Summer savory	Mushrooms, vegetables, quiche	Treats digestive and respiratory issues.
Tarragon	Chicken, fish, vegetables, sauces—"classic French cooking"	Stimulates digestion. Promotes sleep—mildly sedative. Induces menstruation.
Thyme	Soups, stews, tomato-based sauces	May treat infections. Soothes sore throats and hay fever. Can help expel parasites. Relieves minor skin irritations.
Wintergreen	Ice cream, candies, desserts	Strong anti-inflammatory and antiseptic properties. Treats arthritis and rheumatism. Relieves flatulence.
Winter savory	Beans, meats, vegetables	Treats digestive and respiratory issues. Antibacterial properties.
Yarrow	Salad dressings, infused oils	Helps heal minor wounds. Eases menstrual pain and heavy flow. Tonic properties.

Gardening Techniques

Gardeners are creative people who are always on the lookout for the most efficient, interesting, and beautiful ways to grow their favorite plants. Whether you need to save money, reduce your workload, or keep plants indoors, the following gardening techniques are just a sampling of the many ways to grow your very own bountiful garden.

Barrel

Lidless plastic food-grade barrels or drums are set on raised supports. Before the barrel is filled with soil, slits are cut into the sides of the barrel and shaped into pockets. A PVC pipe is perforated with holes and set into the center and out of the bottom of the barrel as a delivery tool for watering, draining, fertilizing, and feeding the optional worm farm.

Strengths

Initial cost is moderate. Retains moisture, warms quickly, drains well, takes up little space, maximizes growing area, and repels burrowing rodents. Little weeding or back-bending required.

Weaknesses

Not always attractive, initially labor intensive, requires special tools to modify. Not generally suited for crops that are deep-rooted, large vining, or traditionally grown in rows, such as corn.

Hügelkultur

These permanent raised beds utilize decomposing logs and woody brush that have been stacked into a pyramidal form on top of the soil's surface or in shallow trenches and then packed and covered with eight to ten inches of soil, compost, and well-rotted manure. The rotting wood encourages soil biota while holding and releasing moisture to plants, much like a sponge. English pronunciation: "hoogle-culture."

Strengths
Vertical form warms quickly, drains well, reduces watering needs, increases overall planting surface, and reduces bending chores. In time the rotting wood breaks down into humus-rich soil.

Weaknesses
Labor-intensive construction and mulch tends to slide down sides. Requires two to three years of nitrogen supplementation, repeated soaking, and filling sunken voids with soil. Voids can also be attractive to rodents and snakes in the first few years.

Hydroponic
Hydroponics is based on a closed (greenhouse) system relying on carefully timed circulation of nutrient-enriched water flowing through a soilless growing medium in which plants grow. Aerial parts are supported above the water by rafts and, at times, vertical supports. With the addition of fish tanks to the system, hydroponics becomes aquaponics.

Strengths
Customizable to any size. Versatile, efficient, productive, and weedless. Produce stays clean.

Weaknesses

Large systems are expensive and complicated to set up and maintain; require multiple inputs of heat, light, and nutrients; and are limited to certain crop types.

Lasagna

Based on sheet composting, lasagna gardens are built up in layers, starting with paper or cardboard that is placed on top of turf-covered or tilled ground to smother weeds and feed ground worm activity. This is then covered in repeating layers of peat moss, compost, leaves, wood chips, manure, and yard waste (green, brown, green), which eventually break down into rich, humusy soil.

Strengths

Excellent natural method to enrich poor soils, utilizes organic waste, supports soil biota, and improves drainage while reducing the need for fertilizers and excessive watering.

Weaknesses

Initially labor intensive and the proper breakdown of bed materials takes months, so is not suited to "quick" gardening. Requires ready and abundant sources of clean, unsprayed, organic materials.

Ruth Stout

This "no work" garden is based on deep, permanent layers of progressively rotting straw mulch, which simultaneously builds soil, feeds plants, blocks weeds, and reduces watering. Seeds and plants are placed into the lower decomposed layers. Fresh straw is added as plants grow and kept at a depth of eight or more inches.

Strengths

No tilling, few weeds, reduced watering and fertilizing. Warms quickly in the spring and prevents winter heaving. An excellent method for rocky, sandy, or clay soils.

Weaknesses

Requires an abundance of straw each season, which can be expensive and difficult to transport, move, and store. Deep mulch may encourage burrowing rodents and provide shelter for slugs, insect pests, and diseases.

Soil Bag

This simple method utilizes one or more twenty- to forty-pound bags of commercial potting soil or topsoil simply laid out flat on turf, mulch, or wood pallets. A rectangular hole is cut into the top and drainage holes are punched through the bottom. A light dusting of fertilizer is mixed in and plants and seeds are sown.

Strengths

Super easy, weed-free, no-till garden and a great way to start an in-ground garden. Fun for kids and those without a yard.

Weaknesses

Limited to shallow-rooted crops, needs consistent watering and fertilizing, and may flood in heavy rains. Cats may find this an attractive litter box.

Straw Bale

One or more square, string-bound straw bales are placed cut side up either directly on the ground or on top of a weed barrier and soaked with water for several days or even months and treated with nitrogen to help speed the decomposition of the straw. Alternatively, bales can be overwintered in place before using. Once ready, bales are parted down the center, filled with soil and compost, and planted with seeds or starts.

Strengths

Good on poor soils, even concrete. No tilling required, few weeds, handicap accessible, versatile, easy to configure, and renter-friendly. Spent bales make excellent mulch.

Weaknesses

Straw bales can be expensive, heavy, and difficult to transport. These gardens can initially be labor intensive, require frequent watering and fertilizing, and must be replaced every one or two seasons. Nitrogen from treated bales can leach into the local environment and affect the watershed.

Square Foot

This modern take on French Intensive gardening utilizes raised beds filled with a special soilless blend enclosed in a box frame that is further divided into twelve-by-twelve-inch squares, or one square foot. Each square is planted or seeded based on the correct spacing requirements of each plant. Large crops, like tomatoes, are planted one to a square, while small crops like radishes are planted sixteen to a square.

Strengths

Proper plant spacing utilizes space, increases yields, and reduces weeds. Adding trellises increases growing capacity. Raised beds drain well, warm quickly, hold mulch, look tidy, and are easy to mow around.

Weaknesses

Initial construction is expensive, labor intensive, and often impermanent. Requires frequent watering in dry spells, and not all crops are suitable. Grids can be tedious to use and do not remove the gardener's need to learn proper plant spacing.

Vertical

Vertical gardens make use of nontraditional gardening space in two ways. The first is by training vining and climbing plants onto trellises, arbors, or fences and growing in raised beds, pots, urns, or tubs. The second is by firmly securing containers, troughs, rain gutters, or vertical garden felt pockets onto permanent frames supported by fences, walls, or other sturdy vertical structures. These gardens are typically irrigated by automatic drip or hydroponic systems. Soilless options are available.

Strengths

Attractive and weed-free indoor-outdoor garden perfect for small yards, renters, and disabled persons. Helps hide ugly structures and views and defines outdoor spaces.

Weaknesses

Construction of large systems and very sturdy structures can be initially expensive or labor intensive. Not conducive to all garden crops and requires frequent and consistent applications of moisture and fertilizer.

2021 Themed Garden Plans

Pollinator Herb Garden

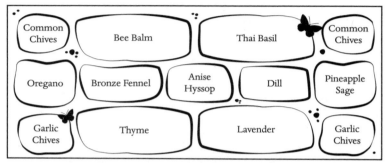

This garden will attract and feed hummingbirds, honey bees, and all kinds and sizes of native bees, wasps, and flies. It will also provide colors, scents, and flavors for the gardener to enjoy. I particularly like the pom-pom flowers of chives—pink for common chives and white for garlic chives—and the tall feathery foliage of dill and fennel. Mix together a couple of different varieties of thyme and lavender to increase bloom time. All these herbs can be grown from seed if you start them early in the season and all (except pineapple sage in colder climates) are perennial or will reseed themselves.

Rainbow Herb Garden

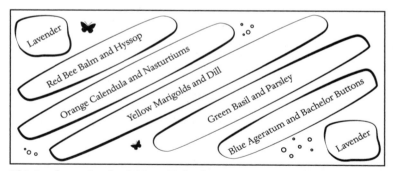

This is a fun garden for children. Each color row can mix together a couple types of plants for variety and to extend the bloom time. There are several deep red varieties of hyssop and bee balm in seed catalogs that are beautiful. My favorite bright orange calendula is 'Ball's Improved Orange'. If you grow from seed, you can get specific varieties, but there are lots of nursery-grown plants of most of these types available for quick and easy planting.

Soup Garden

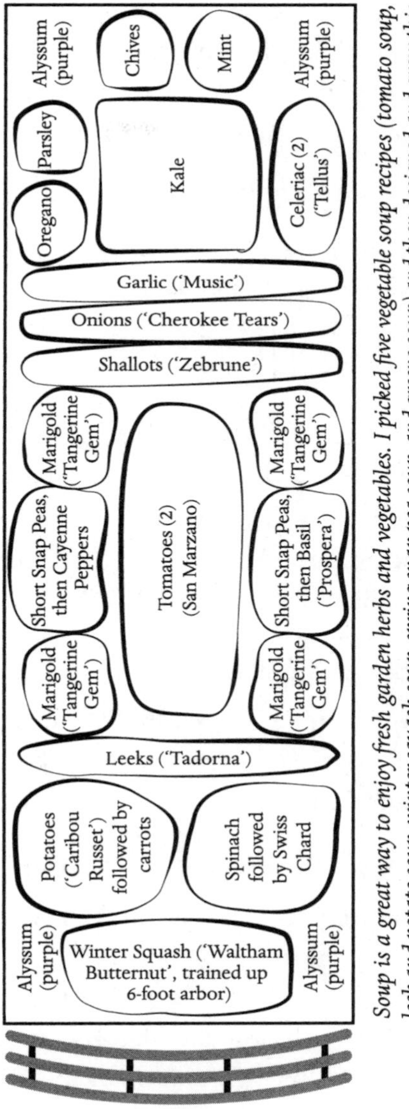

Alyssum (purple)
Chives
Mint
Alyssum (purple)
Parsley
Oregano
Kale
Celeriac (2) ('Tellus')
Garlic ('Music')
Onions ('Cherokee Tears')
Shallots ('Zebrune')
Marigold ('Tangerine Gem')
Marigold ('Tangerine Gem')
Short Snap Peas, then Cayenne Peppers
Tomatoes (2) (San Marzano)
Short Snap Peas, then Basil ('Prospera')
Marigold ('Tangerine Gem')
Marigold ('Tangerine Gem')
Leeks ('Tadorna')
Potatoes ('Caribou Russet') followed by carrots
Spinach followed by Swiss Chard
Alyssum (purple)
Winter Squash ('Waltham Butternut', trained up 6-foot arbor)
Alyssum (purple)

Soup is a great way to enjoy fresh garden herbs and vegetables. I picked five vegetable soup recipes (tomato soup, leek and potato soup, winter squash soup, spring snap pea soup, and greens soup) and then designed and grew this garden with their ingredients. It's designed for a 4 × 14-foot bed with a large arbor at one end. You can read about this garden on page 59. Where there are specific varieties that I particularly like, I have added them to the design.

Planning Your 2021 Garden

Prepare your soil by tilling and fertilizing. Use the grid on the right, enlarging on a photocopier if needed, to sketch your growing space and identify sunny and shady areas.

Plot Shade and Sun

Watch your yard or growing space for a day, checking at regular intervals (such as once an hour), and note the areas that receive sun and shade. This will shift over the course of your growing season. Plant accordingly.

Diagram Your Space

Consider each plant's spacing needs before planting. Vining plants, such as cucumbers, will sprawl out and require trellising or a greater growing area than root crops like carrots. Be sure to avoid pairing plants that naturally compete or harm each other (see the Companion Planting Guide on page 272).

Also consider if your annual plants need to be rotated. Some herbs will reseed, some can be planted in the same place year after year, and some may need to be moved after depleting the soil of certain nutrients during the previous growing season.

Determine Your Last Spring Frost Date

Using data from the previous year, estimate the last spring frost date for your area and note what you'll need to plant before or after this date. Refer to seed packets, plant tags, and experts at your local garden center or University Extension for the ideal planting time for each plant. For information on planting by the moon, see *Llewellyn's 2021 Moon Sign Book*.

My 2021 last spring frost date: _____

Growing Space Grid

☐ = _____ feet

January

To Do	Plants	Dates

Notes:

_____

_____

_____

_____

_____

_____

_____

JANUARY

			🌓		1	2
3	4	5	🌓	7	8	9
10	11	12	🌑	14	15	16
17	18	19	🌗	21	22	23
24	25	26	27	🌕	29	30
31						

Homemade Suet

Suet blocks are easy to make. Melt 1 cup animal fat or nut butter. Add 1 cup each oatmeal and cornmeal. Add bird seed, chopped unsalted nuts, and/or dried fruit to make a thick mix. Pour in a loaf pan and refrigerate until firm. Cut into blocks and use as needed.

February

To Do	Plants	Dates

Notes:

_____

_____

_____

_____

_____

_____

_____

Chickweed Pesto

Chickweed (Stellaria media) *is a landscape pest that makes a tasty pesto. Collect and wash 3 cups of fresh chickweed tops. Process in a food processer. Add 2 cloves garlic and ½ cup olive oil. Add ½ cup each parmesan cheese and pine nuts. Finish with the juice of half a lemon.*

FEBRUARY

1	2	3	◐	5	6
7	8	9	10	●	12	13
14	15	16	17	18	◑	20
21	22	23	24	25	26	○
28						

March

To Do	Plants	Dates

Notes:

_____

_____

_____

_____

_____

_____

_____

<table>
<tr><td colspan="7" align="center">MARCH</td></tr>
<tr><td></td><td>1</td><td>2</td><td>3</td><td>4</td><td>◐</td><td>6</td></tr>
<tr><td>7</td><td>8</td><td>9</td><td>10</td><td>11</td><td>12</td><td>●</td></tr>
<tr><td>14</td><td>15</td><td>16</td><td>17</td><td>18</td><td>19</td><td>20</td></tr>
<tr><td>◑</td><td>22</td><td>23</td><td>24</td><td>25</td><td>26</td><td>27</td></tr>
<tr><td>○</td><td>29</td><td>30</td><td>31</td><td></td><td></td><td></td></tr>
</table>

What and When to Prune

Most broadleaf evergreens and conifers can be pruned now. Plants that will bloom after about July 4 can and should be pruned now. Crepe myrtles, oakleaf hydrangeas, beauty bushes, and chaste trees fall in this category. If the plant blooms in spring, delay pruning until after it flowers.

April

To Do	Plants	Dates

Notes:

_____

_____

_____

_____

_____

_____

_____

Root Hormone Tea for Cuttings

*Make your own rooting hormone from willow
(Salix). Tender young branches work best. Cut 2
cups of stems no thicker than a pencil and 3–4
inches long. Put in a large bucket and cover with
1 gallon of boiling water. Let steep overnight.
Strain and bottle.*

APRIL

				1	2	3
◗ 5	6	7	8	9	10	
● 12	13	14	15	16	17	
18	19	◖ 21	22	23	24	
25	○ 27	28	29	30		

May

To Do	Plants	Dates

Notes:

_____

_____

_____

_____

_____

_____

_____

MAY

						1
2	◑	4	5	6	7	8
9	10	●	12	13	14	15
16	17	18	◐	20	21	22
23	24	25	○	27	28	29
30	31					

Gardening by the Moon

Gardening by the moon means planning garden chores when the moon is in the right phase. Plant crops that fruit above ground when the moon is new or waxing. Plants that form their seeds inside do best when planted in the second quarter of the moon. Plant root crops in the waning moon.

June

To Do	Plants	Dates

Notes:

_____

_____

_____

_____

_____

_____

_____

Staking Tall Flowers
Got a broken spring or fan rake? Turn it upside down and install it in the ground behind your really tall flowers or any vining plants. Tether the plant to the tines as it grows. Before installation, you can spray paint it to stand out or blend in with the rest of your garden.

JUNE

		1	◑	3	4	5
6	7	8	9	●	11	12
13	14	15	16	◓	18	19
20	21	22	23	○	25	26
27	28	29	30			

July

To Do	Plants	Dates

Notes:

_____

_____

_____

_____

_____

_____

_____

JULY

					◗ 2	3
4	5	6	7	8	●	10
11	12	13	14	15	16	◐
18	19	20	21	22	○	24
25	26	27	28	29	30	◑

Proper Lawn Care in Summer

Cool-season grasses like fescue and rye should be allowed to rest in the hottest part of the summer: no fertilizer and keep the spraying for weeds to a minimum. Warm-season grasses like zoysia, centipede, and Bermuda should be monitored for fungal problems. Use fungicides to prevent infection.

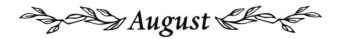

August

To Do	Plants	Dates

Notes:

_____

_____

_____

_____

_____

_____

_____

Keep It, Pot It, or Throw It Out?

As the season ends, you can pot up most annual herbs and move them indoors. If you don't have a sunny window, invest in a grow light. Save unusual annual herbs like blue basil or tropical herbs like patchouli to take cuttings for next season. Just be prepared to nurse your treasure until spring.

AUGUST

1	2	3	4	5	6	7
●	9	10	11	12	13	14
◐	16	17	18	19	20	21
○	23	24	25	26	27	28
29	◑	31				

September

To Do	Plants	Dates

Notes:

_____

_____

_____

_____

_____

_____

_____

SEPTEMBER

			1	2	3	4
5	●	7	8	9	10	11
12	◑	14	15	16	17	18
19	○	21	22	23	24	25
26	27	◐	29	30		

The Harvest Moon

Most people know the full moon in September is called the Harvest Moon. Harvest Moons can come as early as Sept. 8 or as late as Oct. 8. Farmers are said to use the extra light provided by the moon to bring in crops. The "official" Harvest Moon is the one closest to the fall equinox.

October

To Do	Plants	Dates

Notes:

_____

_____

_____

_____

_____

_____

_____

Preparing for Winter Bird Feeding

As winter approaches, check your bird feeders and houses. Make repairs or just toss the old ones and put new ones on your shopping list. Hummingbird feeders should be taken down, cleaned, and put away. Wash feeders with mild, soapy water and allow to dry. Wash your suet feeder too.

OCTOBER

					1	2
3	4	5	●	7	8	9
10	11	◐	13	14	15	16
17	18	19	○	21	22	23
24	25	26	27	◑	29	30
31						

November

To Do	Plants	Dates

Notes:

NOVEMBER

	1	2	3	●	5	6
7	8	9	10	◐	12	13
14	15	16	17	18	○	20
21	22	23	24	25	26	◑
28	29	30				

Bulb Planting Tips

Last chance to get those fall bulbs in the ground! Plant in loose, well-drained soil in a sunny to dappled-shade location. Mix bone meal or bulb fertilizer to the planting area. Plant in odd-numbered groups for a natural look. The planting hole should be 3 times as deep as the bulb is tall. Mulch well.

December

To Do	Plants	Dates

Notes:

_____

_____

_____

_____

_____

_____

_____

Holiday Indoor Plants

Poinsettia, amaryllis, and paperwhite all need bright light (not direct sunlight) to stay compact. Don't overwater, set in drafty spots, or set too close to heating vents. To save seasonal plants over the winter, check with your local cooperative extension service for handy tips.

DECEMBER

					1	2	3 ●
5	6	7	8	9	◐	11
12	13	14	15	16	17	○
19	20	21	22	23	24	25
◑	27	28	29	30	31	

Notes

Contributors

Anne Sala is a freelance writer located in Minnesota. She divides her time between working for her children's school and obsessing about what to make for dinner. A puppy joined her family over the summer, and Anne is thrilled to have another mouth to feed—especially since the dog is proving to be a more adventurous eater than her children.

Annie Burdick is a writer and editor based in Portland, Oregon. She's passionate about the written word and has had writing published in several magazines, journals, and anthologies. She spends much of her spare time reading, playing with her dog, and having adventures around the Pacific Northwest. She can be found at annieburdickfreelance.com. Follow her progress with the full Sandwich Night cookbook on Instagram at @sandwich.night.

Autumn Damiana is an author, artist, crafter, amateur photographer, and regular contributor to Llewellyn's annuals. Along with writing and making art, Autumn has a degree in early childhood education. She lives with her husband and doggy familiar in the beautiful San Francisco Bay Area. Visit her online at www.autumndamiana.com.

Charlie Rainbow Wolf is happiest when she is creating something, especially if it's made from items that others have discarded. Pottery, writing, knitting, astrology, and tarot ignite her passion, but she happily confesses she's easily distracted; life offers such wonderful things to explore! A recorded singer-songwriter and published author, she champions holistic living and lives in the Midwest with her husband and special-needs Great Danes. Astrology reports, smudge pots, smudge blends, and more are available through her website at charlie rainbow.com.

Diana Rajchel lives in San Francisco, where she runs the Emperor Norton Pagan Social and handles the oft-squirrelly city spirit. She is the author of *Urban Magick*, the *Mabon* and *Samhain* books in the Llewellyn Sabbat Essentials series, and the Diagram Prize–nominee *Divorcing a Real Witch*.

Divina Cornick is a writer and yoga instructor living in South Carolina with her dog. She holds a BA in international studies and loves to skydive, read, hike, and garden. She specializes in weaving magic on the yoga mat, bringing movement to the Craft and using the body to focus the mind and ignite the soul. You can follow her adventures on divinacornick .blogspot.com, instagram.com/divinacornick, and instagram .com/yogascopes.

Elizabeth Barrette lives in central Illinois and enjoys magical crafts, historic religions, and gardening for wildlife. She has written columns on Pagan practice, speculative fiction, gender studies, and social and environmental issues. Her book *Composing Magic* explains how to combine writing and spirituality. Visit her blog at ysabetwordsmith.dreamwidth.org.

Holly Bellebuono is an award-winning herbalist, author, and international speaker renowned for teaching, training, and lecturing in Western botanical medicine and self-empowerment. She leads workshops and retreats internationally, lectures at conferences and universities, and directs the Bellebuono School of Herbal Medicine's online and onsite training and certificate programs. Her courses are open to all levels of students and are welcoming, enriching, and inclusive. For more information or to register, visit HollyBellebuono.com.

James Kambos is a writer, artist, and herbalist from Ohio. He developed an interest in herbs and flowers while spending time on his grandparents' farm as a child. His home and garden have been featured on garden tours.

JD Hortwort resides in North Carolina. She is an avid student of herbology and gardening. She has written a weekly garden column since 1991. She is an award-winning author, journalist, and magazine editor and a frequent contributor to the Llewellyn annuals. When not at the keyboard, she spends time in her own landscape, taking trips with friends, and with her nose buried in a book.

Jill Henderson is a backwoods herbalist, author, artist, and world traveler with a penchant for wild edible and medicinal plants, culinary herbs, and nature ecology. She is a longtime contributor to *Llewellyn's Herbal Almanac* and *Acres USA* magazine and is the author of *The Healing Power of Kitchen Herbs, A Journey of Seasons*, and *The Garden Seed Saving Guide*. Visit Jill's blog at www.ShowMeOz.wordpress.com.

Kathy Martin is a Master Gardener and longtime author of the blog *Skippy's Vegetable Garden*, a journal of her vegetable gardens. The blog has won awards including *Horticulture Magazine*'s Best Gardening Blog. She volunteers at gardens including the Massachusetts Horticultural Society's Gardens at Elm Bank. Kathy lives near Boston with her family, dogs, chickens, and bees. She strives to grow all her family's vegetables herself using sustainable organic methods.

Kathy Vilim is a Midwestern girl transplanted to Southern California who writes about the importance of creating outdoor living space using native plants and attracting pollinators. Kathy is a naturalist and photojournalist and finds herself in demand as a garden design consultant. Visit canativegardener .blogspot.com.

Kristen Schuhmann is a wellness writer and herbalist living in Redmond, WA. She specializes in the art and craft of herbalism and gives classes online and in real life. Find her at botanical alchemyandapothecary.com, on Facebook at facebook.com/botanicalalchemyandapothecary, or on Instagram at @botanicalalchemyandapothecary.

Linda Raedisch is a papercrafter, soapmaker, and tea enthusiast and has been writing books and articles for Llewellyn since 2011. You can read more about Egtved Girl and Bronze Age cookery in her latest book, *The Lore of Old Elfland: Secrets from the Bronze Age to Middle Earth*. See her paper creations and other oddities on her Instagram page at @lindaraedisch.

Mireille Blacke, MA, LADC, RD, CD-N, is a registered dietitian, bariatric program coordinator at Saint Francis Hospital, and professor at the University of Saint Joseph in Hartford, Connecticut. Mireille worked in rock radio for two decades before shifting her career to psychology, nutrition, and addiction counseling.

Monica Crosson is the author of *Wild Magical Soul, The Magickal Family,* and *Summer Sage*. She is a Master Gardener who lives in the beautiful Pacific Northwest, happily digging in the dirt and tending her raspberries with her family and their small menagerie of farm animals. Monica is a regular contributor to

Llewellyn's annuals as well as *Enchanted Living Magazine* and *Witchology Magazine*.

Natalie Zaman is the author of *Color and Conjure* and *Magical Destinations of the Northeast*. A regular contributor to various Llewellyn annual publications, she also writes the recurring feature Wandering Witch for *Witches & Pagans* magazine. When not on the road, she's busy tending her magical back garden. Visit Natalie online at nataliezaman.blogspot.com.

Rachael Witt is a community herbalist, gardener, and ancestral skills teacher in the Pacific Northwest. She is the founder of Wildness Within, an herbal business that offers plant-based classes and workshops, handmade products, and herbal consultations. She has a degree in ecology and evolution biology with an emphasis in plant ecology. Rachael teaches people how to connect with place and their well-being through gardening, processing, and wild-tending. Learn more at WildnessWithin Living.com.

Sandra Kynes is a Reiki practitioner and a member of the Bards, Ovates and Druids. She likes to develop unique views and methods to explore the world, which serve as the basis for her many books. She has lived in New York City, Europe, England, and now coastal New England. She loves connecting with nature through gardening, hiking, bird-watching, and ocean kayaking. Visit her website at kynes.net.

Susan Pesznecker is a mother, writer, nurse, and college English professor living in the beautiful Pacific Northwest with her poodles. An initiated Druid, green magick devoteé, and amateur herbalist, Sue loves reading, writing, cooking, travel, and anything having to do with the outdoors. Previous works include *Crafting Magick with Pen and Ink, The Magickal Retreat,* and *Yule: Recipes & Lore for the Winter Solstice.* She's a regular contributor to the Llewellyn annuals. Follow her on Instagram at @SusanPesznecker.

Suzanne Ress runs a small farm in the Alpine foothills of Italy, where she lives with her husband. She has been a practicing Pagan for as long as she can remember and was recently featured in the exhibit "Worldwide Witches" at the Hexenmuseum of Switzerland. She is the author of *The Trial of Goody Gilbert.*

Thea Fiore-Bloom, PhD, is a humor-loving, award-winning journalist, artist, and children's literacy volunteer. She holds a doctorate in mythology with an emphasis in depth psychology. Check out her new blog, *The Charmed Studio.* It's a sanctuary for creatives who care about soul. Thea's dream is to help creatives like you feel better, write better, and sell better—by being yourself.

Vannoy Gentles Fite is a certified herbalist, aromatherapist, Ayurvedic life coach, and a student of everything. Fite has published three books: *Healing with Essential Oils, Essential Oils for Emotional Wellbeing,* and *Llewellyn's Book of Natural Remedies.* She lives in Texas surrounded by her beautiful family. Fite enjoys studying natural healing methods and believes fully that the plants provided on earth are the answers to humankind's needs.

Gardening Resources

Cooking with Herbs and Spices compiled by **Susan Pesznecker**
Gardening Techniques written by **Jill Henderson**
2021 Themed Garden Plans designed by **Kathy Martin**
2021 Gardening Log tips written by **JD Hortwort**